# CONDUCTING BASELINE STUDIES

## *in*

# POST CONFLICT SETTINGS:

LEARNING FROM EXPERIENCE OF THE
EAST OF THE DEMOCRATIC REPUBLIC OF CONGO

Olivier Mumbere Muhongya

Order this book online at www.trafford.com
or email orders@trafford.com

Most Trafford titles are also available at major online book retailers.

The author is currently a USAID-DRC employee. However, this was prepared in his
personal capacity and on his personal time, and the views expressed in this publication
do not necessarily reflect the views of the United States Agency for International
Development or the United States Government.

Printed in the United States of America.

ISBN: 978-1-4669-7147-9 (sc)
ISBN: 978-1-4669-7146-2 (e)

*Trafford rev. 06/06/2013*

 www.trafford.com

**North America & international**
toll-free: 1 888 232 4444 (USA & Canada)
phone: 250 383 6864 ♦ fax: 812 355 4082

# Contents

For Marie-Josephine my beloved wife.

For Olive, Gloria, and Michelange my dear children.

# Acronyms

**ACOPLAKA**: Association Communitaire des Planteurs de Kasugho, local association in Kasugho involved in plantation;

**ADBC**: Agent de Distribution à Base Communautaire; persons trained by JGI to distribute contraceptive tools (methods) into villages;

**BS**: Baseline Study

**CACUDEKI**: Centre d'Animation pour la Culture et le Développement de Kirumba; local development NGO in Lubero;

**CAF**: Common Assistance Framework

**CARITAS**: a Catholic Organisation involved in emergencies aid;

**CBCA**: Communauté Baptiste au Centre de l'Afrique (Presbytarian Church);

**CBCE**: Communauté Baptiste au Congo Est (Presbytarian Church);

**CCC:** Community-Centered Conservation (Program)

**CEPROSAN**: Centre de Promotion Socio sanitaire; Local NGO involved in water sanitation, protection of the environment etc. . . ;

**CSMBUHI**: Complexe Scolaire de Mbuhi; a secondary school located in Mbuhi;

**DRC**: Democratic Republic of the Congo

**FEC:** Fédération des Entreprises du Congo; association of small Entreprises with in Kasugho village;

**FRATERNITE**: in English FRATERNITY, an association of solidarity in Mbuhi village;

**GDRC**: Government of the Democratic Republic of the Congo

**ICDP**: Integrated Conservation and Development Project

**IDP**: Internal Displaced People

**JGI**: The Jane Goodall Institute

**MDGs**: Millennium Development Goals

**ORPALU**: Organisation des Planteurs de Lubero; local NGO involved in agriculture in Lubero Territory;

**PAP**: Priority Action Program

**PMP:** Performance Management Plan

**PRSP**: Poverty Reduction Strategy Paper

**PRGSP**: Poverty Reduction and Growth Strategy Paper

**PS**: Poste de Santé (Dispensary).

**RGT**: Réserve des Gorilles de Tayna

**UGADEC**: Union des Associations pour la Conservation des Gorilles et le développement à l'Est du Congo

**USAID**: United States Agency for International Development

# INTRODUCTION

T he global economy today is subject of heightened levels of uncertain. In developed countries, these uncertainties are fuelled by the economic crisis while in developing countries poverty and the incident of civil conflicts are to blame. While donor countries are forced adopt austerity measures, they find themselves in the moral obligation to address the poverty which in conflict ridden areas affect the most vulnerable. These difficult budget allocation decisions have prompted donors to target their activities to evidence proven solutions. Donors have, henceforth, increased their expenditure on monitoring and evaluation activities to help both justify their development activities and increase the value for money in development expenditures.

Donor governments and international institutions are emphasising on proving measurable results from aid programs, increasing oversight; and designing more and more metrics to track programs implementation. European and North American governments are, more than before, seeking to improve the effectiveness of development resources. It's clear that new policies that will oversee aid for development could lead to better planning and management of scarce resources with stronger focus on results. This will certainly boost legislative oversight but also evaluation by development practitioners. The eminent danger of this trend could be the excessive focus on quantitative indicators which at times can be biased by political instabilities. Evidences of improvements due to development aid should be proved by rigorous evaluation and such evaluation must come from well-designed baseline studies. But the challenge is on how to conduct sound baseline studies within fragile countries emerging from conflict situation? The large influx of development funds in post-conflict countries from a large number of heterogeneous donors can in fact bias. In addition, the high incidence of migration and change of institutions can further increase the number of confounders.

The Democratic Republic of the Congo is difficultly emerging from two decades of war situation. Yet, its eastern side is experiencing security unrest due to the continuous presence of various militia and rebel groups on its territory. In North and South Kivu alone, armed rebel and government forces currently exceed 20, 000 persons. Since 2005, the UN Mission in Congo has documented 80,000 reported cases of sexual violence in South Kivu alone. These systematic acts of violence traumatize populations and have irrevocably harmful repercussions. Local populations feel powerless to curve the situation, and still desperately abandoned to international aid.

The DRC situation is similar to the one experienced by population in Iraq, Sudan or Afghanistan. What's common in these settings? The idea behind this book is to point out similarities of post conflict settings in order to find out ways of addressing the issue of conducting baseline studies. Baseline studies are the foundation of any serious monitoring and evaluation systems. However, this starting point is usually skipped out due to various reasons among them the security unrest. In fact, we believe that command and control systems of funding provided to post conflict countries have development consequences in post conflict environments. The usual output data provided by development practitioners are becoming limited, unable to provide significant information.

The book concludes showing that despite the security concerns and all other uncertainties that traditionally surround post conflict settings, development measurements still compulsory due to current economic downturn. Such measurements should be built upon sound and rigorous baseline studies. The latter may serve as the basement for sound donor coordination in post conflict settings like the DRC.

# CHAPTER I

# COMMON FEATURES OF POST CONFLICT COUNTRIES

For the purposes of this book, we'll limit our understanding of conflict to civil war. Civil war is defined as an internal conflict with at least 1, 000 combat-related deaths per year, with both an identifiable rebel organization and government forces suffering at least five percent of these fatalities[1].

It's obvious that any negative Impact that applies to civil war situation fits perfectly in serious conflicts which are deemed more devastative.

## 1.  Countries deemed most at risk and Instable

Poorly equipped in rule of law system, post conflict countries are instable in a sense that they still likely to experience coups d'Etat and other types of illegal or unpredictable political succession; breakdown of political, economic, and social institutions; systemic corruption; widespread organised crime; loss of territorial control; economic crisis; wide-scale public unrest; involuntary mass population displacement; and violent internal or international conflict/involvement.

The risk derives from mismanagement or political manipulation and rent seeking behaviour. The lack of consensus or weak

---

[1]     Collier Paul and Anke Hoeffler, 2004, *"Green and grievance in civil war"*, Oxford Economic Papers, 56(4): 563-595.

consensus among the most influential groups at the out set of the post conflict era can also play a catalytical role in post conflict situations. Besides, some factors can be also causes of instability and consequences of instability. Poverty, economic decline, natural resource dependence, and a bad regional neighbourhood are strong factors that may fuel instability.

Basically, instability will be subject to country capacity and resilience, risk factors for instability, external stabilizing factors, feedback loop of instability into the risk factors and shocks.

In an effort to address the instability of country, it's necessary to understand what truly drives political instability along with its consequences of poor economic performance and violent conflict.

## 2. Weak macro economic aggregates

### 2.1. General Settings

Civil wars have direct negative Impact on country's natural and human resources, physical infrastructure, housing, education, health facilities, and social capital.

In civil war situation, military spending would increase at the detriment of social sectors including education, health, and infrastructure. In fact, all assets are shifted away from domestic investment.[2]

---

[2]    Collier Paul, ***Risk and Investment in Africa***, 2000, Paul Collier and Catherine Pattillo Basingstoke, Macmillan and New York, St Martin's Press,

- **GDP growth**: there is a vast array of economies' reactions in post conflict periods. A study led upon the recovery of six countries including Sierra Leone, Ethiopia, Mozambique, Cambodia, El Salvador, and Guatemala has demonstrated that countries whose growth was devastated had a strong initial rebound when large aid inflows and a good package of reform catalyzed economic recovery (Rwanda, Bosnia). However, countries that were less damaged by war, growth surges are less intense. In fact, as the latter experienced less aid inflows, their economic growths were not as stronger as for the countries that experienced devastating wars.[3]

Any "rubber band" effect should be considered in its exact context of post conflict as the magnitude of the rebound expressed through percentages can mislead. One should always question the way to go compared to the way the country comes from. Usually, countries come from less than "zero" point.

- **Investment and Capital Stock**: in wartime, these aggregates would deteriorate including infrastructure such as roads, houses and ports. Data show that gross investment as percentage of GDP is very low, on average, during war, particularly where conflict is extensive. But, on average, the investment rate rises by more than 5 percent of GDP during the first five years of recovery. Most of the rise due to aid—financed infrastructure, and/or, in resource—rich countries,

---

[3]    Nathan Associates, 2009, *Patterns of Post conflict Economic Recovery*, Report for USAID Agency, p. 5.

a surge in private investment. Again, situations will vary from one country to another[4].

-   **Inflation**: By its nature, war renders usual livelihoods unaffordable and most of the time disrupts networks that could link centers of consumption to centers producing agricultural items. As a result, the price of staple food may spike. Besides, the large presence of IDPs worsens the situation by exposing population to extensive outbreaks.

## 2.2. Snap shot on the DRC struggling to reach the Completion point of the PRGF5:

The International Monetary Fund (IMF) slowed down on approving the Poverty Reduction and Growth Facility Program (PRGFP) of the Government of the Democratic Republic of Congo (GDRC). In 2006, a program, known in French acronym as PEG (Expansion Program of the Government), was suspended by the IMF, due to excess fiscal slippages. The IMF monitored macroeconomic indicators as well as key structural reforms before coming up with PRGFP. In March, a team of experts from the IMF visited DRC (Democratic Republic of Congo), and had discussions with key government officials and the civil society, to assess ongoing economic situation. In fact, DRC macroeconomic indicators deteriorated given the global economic slowdown and increasing military expenditures due to rebellious activities in the Nord Kivu and South Kivu provinces. For the first

---

[4]    Idem, p. 7.

[5]    DRC reached the completion point in 2010. This section shows how tough was the process which started back in 2001 when President Kabila took over power in DRC.

time since President Joseph Kabila took over power in 2002, DRC has been battling with grave liquidity challenges, due to the shrinking Foreign Currency Reserve, which could not cover importations. In order to get things clearer, the IMF delayed the new agreement that could provide the GDRC with substantial financial means to confront social challenges, exasperated by a fragile post conflict situation. If this situation continued, DRC could have faced acute civil unrest.

The IMF team acknowledged that the continued decline in key export commodity prices has taken a toll on economic activity. Coupled with security and humanitarian spending, this situation has led to fiscal slippages and unleashed pressure on the exchange rate. The 6 percent growth rate in 2008 was blamed on a slowdown in mining and construction activities. Annual inflation fell to 28 percent in December, reflecting a decline in world prices for petroleum and food, while international reserves fell to a five-year low.

As a key result of discussion between the IMF team and the GDRC, the GDRC lowered its forecasts for 2009. Economic growth was projected at 2.5 percent and inflation for the year was expected to be 25 percent. With revenues below expectations and expenditures on the rise, the financing gap was projected to widen significantly. The government was implementing corrective measures and seeking additional concessional external financing consistent with macroeconomic stability and debt sustainability.

The IMF did not show clear position with regards to a Chinese deal, in which DRC was expecting the construction of new infrastructures (Schools, hospitals, roads, and social houses) to be paid off by tons of copper and cobalt, valued at USD9 billion. The GDRC put all it efforts in the implementation of the Chinese deal deemed crucial due to president Kabila's promises during the 2006 campaign. IMF experts, however, considered this Chinese loan as non-concessional, and urged for its review.

### 3.  Poor Business Environment

Various factors would pin down the business environment such as the lack of sound transportation means, telecommunication or banking system. The instability of key macroeconomic indicators does not open horizons for sound and realistic planning among economic operators. Such situation affects the basic services of banks especially the credit granting.

The absence of rule of law along with the "attempts and failures" of the government in setting up the fiscal policy may prompt in the contraction of businesses. The new order may be found stringent by some economic operators who will choose to develop their activities in the black market or in the informal sector. As military operations would still going on, the government will be confronted to making tough choices of increasing taxes without clearly proving returns to populations. Aid inflow is critical in supporting one government's effort.

### 4.  Poverty and Inequality

Poverty understood as the absence of regular and sufficient income is widespread in post conflict settings. In fact, the disruption of livelihoods and the uncertainty that features such period are factors that maintain population under dire poverty. Though factors of production are available, the conflict situation does not allow them to get into the process of production due to insecurity. Besides, even when salaries exist, their purchasing power will be eroded due to various reasons including the inflation, the levelling down phenomenon as a handful of salary holders will have to take on their own the needs of many idle workers in large families.

The above points four and five are intertwined when it comes to explain capital inflow in a given country. The paradox of capital inflow has proven that "*capital does not seem to flow to those nations where it should be most valuable. Instead of capital-rich countries to capital-poor countries, we often observe the opposite for two reasons:*

- *Differences among nations other than their accumulation. In fact, compared to rich nations, poor nations may have less access to advanced technologies, lower levels of education (due to war situation), or less efficient economic policies.*

- *Property rights are often not enforced: corruption is typically much higher; revolutions; coups, and expropriation of wealth are more common; and governments often default on their debts. So even if capital is more valuable in poor nations, foreigners may avoid investing their wealth there simply because they are afraid of losing it. Moreover, local investors face similar incentives*"[6].

All the above factors show how critical is the aid inflow in post conflict environments. Fresh money from rich countries

---

[6] Mankiw Gregory: ***"Macroeconomics",*** Worth Publishers, New York, 2007, p. 130-131

is needed and appear to be the unique way to jump start or at lest to help these weak economies to move toward a situation of recovery and later on even to sustainable growth. Without aid inflow, all the effort aiming at consolidating peace may result in tough setbacks.

# Chapter II

# Economic Down Turn Versus Aid Effectiveness

I t's paramount to understand how the current economic crisis came in. In fact, understanding the origin of this economic crisis may help to understand the consequences of this crisis upon aid management. As rich countries are willing to continue supporting poor countries, they all have evoked their readiness to better manage this aid. More clearly, they would be likely more a keen to exert more control as to the impact or effectiveness of their funds.

## 1. Economic Down turn

### 1.1. Origin of the crisis

All well intentioned historians of economy agree on the fact that the economic down has its roots in the World financial system. Unlike the most recent world economic crisis of the seventies, the current economic down is the result of internal chocks.

The current crisis has its origin in the high risk mortgaged loan market of in the United States designed "sub primes". Behind the sub primes crisis laid the belief that the financial market could return to its equilibrium position automatically. This big mistake prompted the Lehman Brothers along with other actors of the American financial system in a situation of bankruptcy. In fact, financial institutions were unable to provide loans to economic operators who could not pay back their debts.

Despite western governments' commitment to protect the system from expanding the cancer across the system, countries at the periphery were already unable to protect themselves. In fact, the latter could not present credible guaranties. Therefore, capitals run away from east-European countries, Asia, and Latin American. All currencies fall down compared to dollar and yen. The exchange rates of many raw materials fall down and interest rates spiked in emerging countries. The crisis left the financial terrain and evolved in an economic one affecting human resources in unprecedented way.

Factors that played catalytic role for the crisis, and which brought in complexities are the following:

- **Lack of regulation**: financial markets were fully involved into speculative activities for decades. The higher was the risk the more the game was capable to drag rewarding yields. Hence the bubble took very excessive and speculative trends.

- **Nobody helped to keep speculative bubble into reasonable limits**: prices became the reflections of realities that were no longer under economic operators' control. This resulted in vicious prejudices and irrational anticipations. Governments were called to exert tight control not only on the money supply but also the credit market.

- **Lack of professionalism in the banking/financial system**: the banking system with its complicated connections worldwide has lost its exigencies of coverage and compliance with banking standards. Such rules were in enforcement back in the fifties and sixties.

- **Complexity of innovated financial products**: the steady running toward new financial products did not allow control. Moreover, it rendered useless any attempt to set in place control tools. Governments should have imposed the registration of new financial products prior to get them exchanged on the financial markets.

Efforts aiming at stabilizing the international financial market have not yet proved to be productive. Therefore, salary holders, investors, and producers are therefore still experiencing traumatizing effects of the crisis. Nobody can predict with a maximum of certainty the twist of the on-going crisis.

### 1.2. Level of the Havoc Among Economies

The intention of this paper is not to use figures in order to show how ravaging has been the on-going crisis. Nor its focus is to compare the degree of consequences between countries of the center compared to those in the periphery. For objectivity reasons, the paper would limit its demonstration through the critical equation of any open economy that presents as follow:

**Y-C-G-I=0 or I= Y-C-G**

This identity leads to the concept of saving. In fact, I is the output that remains after the demands of consumers and tthe government have been satisfied. And this remaining part of the national income constitutes the portion that a country may allocate to investment. That why Investment equals to saving. However, we can distinguish two types of savings:

$$S=I=(Y-T-C) + (T-G)$$

The term (Y-T-C) is disposable income minus consumption, which is private saving. The term (T-G) is government revenue minus government spending, which is public saving. Obviously, if government spending exceeds government revenue, the government runs a budget deficit, and public saving is negative. National saving is, therefore, the sum of private and public saving. If the private saving depends mainly on the level of private revenue and private decisions on consumption, the public saving is tributary to government purchases and exogenous variables set by fiscal policymakers.

It becomes easier now to understand that decisions of policymakers of the countries located in the center will be more likely driven by the willingness to address the problems posed by the financial crisis later on converted into real economic depression. For these countries, budget cuts will be obvious and adjustments will be made on government revenue expectations. Budget lines destined to funding development actions were reconsidered and where development funding was maintained, policymakers on both sides of the Atlantic appealed for tight management of the aid or simply made recommendations urging for more accountability and effectiveness of the aid.

Developing countries will certainly be hit by the world economic downturn indirectly, and through various channels.

One of these is the lack of final decision on neither their natural resources nor on the prices of the products their import from developed countries. Some of these products are so critical (fuel) that they will impact negatively developing countries' vulnerable economies. Mme Lagarde, the IMF Director, has already predicted the worst for the African economies for the FY 2012.

Last, but not least, this economic downturn has revealed that many countries of the center (in Europe) were living beyond their real possibilities. And this results in incapacity to meet debt services. This jeopardizes the application of provisions of some treaties due to lack of harmonization of fiscal discipline. The European Union is even on the verge of falling apart.

### 1.3. Potential Aftermaths of the Crisis

In a situation of financial crisis doubled with an economic down turn, the situation of poor countries is getting weaker than ever since developing countries are the most hit by the worst effects of the crisis. The number of poor people in US has doubled even tripled since the beginning of the crisis. For the first time, Europe has experienced demonstrations of young idle people organized in the most ever unified movements of protesters called "indignados". As said here above, the European Union is even on the verge of splitting along with the death of the "euro" money.

Following could be the consequences of this down turn:

-   **Emergence of a new community of donor countries across the world**: the current economic down turn is designing a new distribution of power among countries. At the end of the cyclical crisis, some countries will become richer than others. As a result, new donors will emerge with their new package of conditions for accessing their funding supports. One of these conditions could be capacity to prove outstanding management for impact.

- **More appeal to Accountability as constituency bodies will be very demanding as to the way their tax payers' money will be spent through cooperation agencies**: it's certain that if western countries will have to continue using tax payers' money for development, project implementing organizations will have to be more accountable than ever on the money to be disbursed. Objectives to be set would be clearer, and tools for tracking their achievements would be thoroughly refurbished;

- **Emergence of new Social Entrepreneurs for development actions**: as public funds will be scarce, Social Enterprises will develop new ways of raising funds for addressing well identified social needs. Social Enterprises will be scrutinized with the lenses of the private sectors' taxation bodies. This would result in potential taxation of social enterprises.

- **New Partnerships for addressing development challenges**: It's predictable that developing countries would regroup their development actions. This may bring in more centralization of western countries already enjoying good relationship based upon security cooperation, cultural cooperation etc.

- **Innovative tools for Managing for Impact and Sustainability**: donor countries have already taken distance with some metrics that simply aim at disclosing the traceability of money provided through bilateral cooperation. Output indicators are good, but still mute at certain level. They have to be complemented with a new set of impact and sustainability indicators. For the sake of impact and sustainability poor countries will be demanded to track aggregated indicators at the level of their nations.

- **Evolution towards more coordinated development actions**: Post conflict settings are featured as the most unable to coordinate as quickly as possible donor communities' actions within the needy country. Because of the crisis context, developed countries will put in place mechanisms that may ensure better coordination of development interventions for averting sprinkling of scarce resources for the better and quicker improvement of populations' welfare.

## 2. Aid Effectiveness

Following the above considerations, aid effectiveness would more likely improve in the current context of economic down turn doubled with financial crisis. It's worth mentioning, at this stage of the discussion, that DRC donors still have a long way to make their assistance more effective to the DRC.

In fact, DRC donors are fully committed to establishing a more coordinated assistance strategy. Thematic groups have proven to be effective in pushing various actors to work together, but no detailed information has been made available regarding their respective outputs. Neither the results framework nor the logical framework is known for each thematic group.

The GDRC still have to provide more leadership in this sector by supplying donors with a clear roadmap towards the achievement of its key goals. Donor support is still linked more to the donors' own strategies than to the one put forward by the GDRC. This situation results in serious flaws in donor coordination area. In fact, many projects implemented in the country suffer from following factors pointed out by the African Development Bank: Poor culture of managing for results on the DRC Government side; poor coordination of official development assistance in order to improve its effectiveness; and weak ownership of projects in order to accelerate their implementation[7]. In addition, the existence of hidden or classified agendas or interventions documents is still counterproductive, and may hinder full coordination of the assistance in the future[8].

Thanks to the Minister Olivier Kamitatu (Minister of Planning from 2008 through 2012) leadership who strived to put in place the Kinshasa Agenda declaration and organized donors in clusters, some outcomes are being noticed. For instance, the agriculture sector has established its database providing a basis for who-do-what-where. If this is critical outcome for the cluster, a long way still to be done to instil

---

[7]  *African Development Bank: Mid-term Review of the Results-based Country Strategy Paper, 2018-2012, April 2010*

[8]  *Sylvie More and Megan Price: "The EU's Support to Security System Reform in the Democratic Republic of the Congo: perceptions from the field in spring 2010", May 2011.*

in the cluster a real result-managing approach based on co-funded baseline studies in specific areas.

The DRC, along with its major donors including the United States and United Kingdom, are signatories to the recent Busan Declaration. This is likely to facilitate discussion with a clear focus on addressing the DRC's vulnerabilities. Again, there is a major gap between the declaration and its implementation.

# CHAPTER III

# DRC GOVERNEMENT STRUGGLING TO COORDINATE DONORS[9]

T here is no major study covering the topic of donor coordination in the Democratic Republic of Congo (DRC). The bulk of the information is found among donor reports in the last five years. Among the most relevant in this field are: African Development Bank, DRC Ministry of Planning, European Union, United Nations Development Program, and the World Bank.

## 1. Literature agreement on DRC Donor Coordination

All the reports and studies agree that donor coordination is a well-documented challenge in the DRC. They are also unanimous in acknowledging that very few improvements have been made in some specific sectors, such as the agricultural sector. Thus, much is still to be done before effective coordination is achieved. Moreover, it is worth noting that several studies mention that the GDRC refers to the PRSP with an emphasis on "growth"—making the acronym "PRGSP"—while donors still are not referring to the growth

---

[9] Compiled from following documents: Government of the DRC, Ministry of Planning: Kinshasa Agenda and Government of the DRC: Ministry of Planning, "*Les Groupes Thématiques en Bref*" (2011)

aspect in their reports. This seems to indicate that the GDRC's expectations are higher than the donors.

## 2. Recent Developments

Under the leadership of Mr Olivier Kamitatu, the Government of the Democratic Republic of the Congo made large strides in improving donor coordination. He put in place thematic groups, which have created a new dynamic in the donor community (there are 20 groups today). This has resulted in the revision of the country's Poverty Reduction Strategy Paper. Minister Kamitatu publicized the second generation of the PRSP on November 2, 2011. This PRSP II is a results-based paper aligned to the MDGs with a clear agenda for addressing long run poverty.

The International Community provides strong support through diplomatic, humanitarian, and development assistance. International investment in the Congo reached more than 14 billion USD between 2007 and 2010.

However, every donor is still following their own strategic framework, despite the above achievement. For example, among EU partners, security sector reform has suffered during the last five years from the lack of coordination. In this field, the European Commission has acknowledged the lack of a singular and uniformly-backed policy or strategy to which all the EU actors adhere. Field actors have made little reference to an overarching common EU strategy for supporting security sector reform in the DRC. Nor has there been a clear leading EU figure to align and direct the various EU actors working in the field. So each EU actor in DRC has been intervening based on their own agendas. In addition, this situation has presented a dichotomy between political actors and field staff regarding the European security agenda in the Democratic Republic of Congo.

After the PRSP-I, DRC donors whose aid represented eighty five percent of the assistance to the country developed a Common Assistance Framework (CAF, 2008-2010) for DRC. CAF partners included the World Bank, the European Commission, the International Monetary Fund, the United Nations System, Belgium, Canada, France, Germany, Japan, China, the Netherlands, Sweden, UK, and US. This joint effort was meant to coordinate donor support for the implementation of the DRC Government's Poverty Reduction Strategy Paper of the first generation. The CAF provided an analysis of the country context and the risks of providing development assistance in DRC. It described how the CAF partners will contribute to implementing the five PRSP pillars on Governance, Growth, Social sectors, HIV/AIDS and Community Dynamics. Besides, CAF included a joint results matrix. The Government of DRC endorsed the CAF, and used it to formulate its own short-term priority action plan *("Plan d'Action Prioritaire")*.

The conclusions of the PRSP-I and the mid-term review of the Country Assistance development partners confirmed the relevance of the strategic orientation of the PRSP-I and the Priority Action Programme (PAP). All these documents were used during the drafting of the PRSP of second generation as the donor community anticipated that DRC would face the same challenges identified during the PRSP-I.

The Kinshasa Agenda was the key outcome of the National High Level Forum on Aid Effectiveness held by the Government of Congo from June 15-16, 2011 in Kinshasa. The Forum aimed at engaging the Government of Congo, Development partners, and Civil Society Organizations on practical steps for enhancing aid effectiveness. To this end, the forum considered following topics: aid distribution and appropriateness; mechanisms and programs' implementing tools within priority sectors; and aid architecture. The Forum was aligned to a series of international initiatives including the MDGs.

The Kinshasa Agenda was a "mini-version" of the Paris Declaration for the DRC, and was endorsed by all donors. It was welcomed by donors as a good starting point for harmonizing between the Technical and Financial Partners at the strategic level. Even so, this framework has not always prevented the multiplication and dispersal of activities. In order to operationalize the Kinshasa Agenda, Minister Kamitatu established twenty thematic groups. Thematic groups' productivity varied from one sector to another. The agricultural sector, for example, has been able to produce a sectorial database thanks to technical and financial partners' support. This database should be sustainably managed by government technical services, and serve as the basis for sectorial monitoring and evaluation. However, other thematic groups did not achieve such successes. The uneven results of the thematic groups across the spectrum prompted the Minister of Planning to launch an assessment of the implementation of the revitalization framework of the thematic groups. Following its agenda, this assessment's overall goal will be aimed at reviewing the operational framework and effectiveness of the thematic groups.

Several factors have hindered the GDRC's attempts to exert more effective leadership over donors' interventions in the

DRC. These include: donors' focus on seeking more financial resources rather than on operations in the field; lack of clear engagement on the humanitarian and development agendas on the GDRC's side; and donors' preference of pursuing their own agendas.

Lastly, the PRSP II has been welcomed by the donor community as a key contribution in the GDRC's attempts to curb poverty by using measurable indicators. This results-based programmatic tool should serve as a basis for the GDRC's self-assessment.

### 3.   Major knowledge gaps

All donors are fully committed to establishing a more coordinated assistance strategy. Thematic groups have proven to be effective in pushing various actors to work together, but no detailed information has been made available regarding their respective outputs. Neither the results framework nor the logical framework is known for each thematic group. A publication that encompasses all the above details and that is widely distributed would be a good step toward strengthening unity across the donor community.

### 4.   Major deficiencies in this field by the DRC Government

The GDRC still has to provide more leadership in this sector by supplying donors with a clear roadmap towards the achievement of its key goals. Donor support is still linked more to the donors' own strategies than to the one put forward by the GDRC. This situation results in serious flaws in donor coordination area. In fact, many projects implemented in the country suffer from following factors pointed out by the African Development Bank: Poor culture of managing for results on the DRC Government side; poor coordination of official development assistance in order to improve its effectiveness; and weak ownership of projects in order to accelerate their implementation.

In addition, the existence of hidden or classified agendas or interventions documents is still counterproductive, and may hinder full coordination of the assistance in the future.

The GDRC's incapacity to address good governance issues across all sectors, combined with impunity and security problems on the one hand, and the lack of a clear roadmap on the other hand, will complicate donor coordination.

## 5. Special Opportunities to make advancements in the next five years

Rather than paralyzing DRC decision makers, current problems that the DRC is facing constitute a good basis for facilitating frank discussion between the GDRC and its humanitarian and development partners. These problems include flaws in the electoral process, insecurity, corruption and mismanagement, and dire poverty across the country. These issues offer windows of opportunities for a dialogue between the GDRC and donors. A clear matrix showing which donors are doing which activities and in which location should be re-activated.

## 6. DRC Struggling to meet the Millennium Development Goals

After the implementation of its Country Assistance Strategy (from 2009 through 2011), the USAID DRC Mission is planning to step in a new five year strategy called "Country Development Cooperation Strategy" to run from 2012 through 2017. While this endeavour is ambitious due to the current situation of the country, which is still struggling with war and security volatility issues and mismanagement, it questions the country's improvements toward the Millennium Development Goals by the 2015 horizon.

Such an exercise cannot be done without providing retrospective insights on the DRC Mission's achievements during the last past three years. The exercise becomes even exciting when it comes to establishing comparisons with MDGs' landmarks.

The MDGs entail eight international development goals that 193 governments and 23 international organizations agreed to achieve by the year 2015. The DRC is one of the country signatories of this agreement. The MDGs focus on achieving the following goals: 1) end poverty and hunger eradication; 2) realize universal education; 3) enhance gender equality; 4) improve child health; 5) improve maternal Health; 6) combat HIV/AIDS; 7) increase environmental sustainability; and 8) create global partnerships.

The MDGs aim at improving socioeconomic conditions in the world's poorest. Due to its particular context, the DRC cannot achieve all the eight MDGs by 2015. The donor community task force that was commissioned to work on

DRC's capabilities to achieve the MDGs made three categories of MDGs: those which the DRC was likely to meet by 2015; those which are still potentially achievable; and those that are unlikely to be achieved by 2015.

Like other developing countries, the DRC is still struggling to meet the MDGs by 2015. The DRC is not in a good position to meet following goals: ensuring full employment (1B), realizing universal education (2A); reducing maternal mortality (5A); combatting HIV/AIDS (6A, 6B); integrate the principles of environmental sustainability (7A); and enhancing the lives of people living in slums (7C).

Despite its rich endowments, the DRC is facing tremendous challenges of governance. Poor governance has become a real cross-cutting issue that deprives the country from financial resources. Therefore, key ministries called to invest in social sectors have been unable to deliver measurable results. Young people in the DRC's big cities are the most affected by idleness. The 1-2-3 survey conducted by UNICEF-DRC has revealed that 32 percent of youth are affected by idleness, which is substantially above the national average of 18. 00 percent. The country is plagued by long-running food insecurity.

In general, the literacy rate is lower among women (58.8 percent) than men (85.8 percent). This difference is worse in rural area where gaps between both sexes may vary between 20 to 30 percent. However, in urban area this difference is between 10 to 15 percent. The current trend is good in terms of improvement of the literacy rate for both sexes, but much still to be done[10].

---

[10]   Op. cit., p. 29.

Most of the DRC women work in the agricultural sector. Only 34 percent of them work outside of the agricultural sector. Despite the recognition of some rights, the situation of women is still wretched. Furthermore, despite the improvement of enrolment of girls in primary and secondary schools, the number of girls in schools is still lower than boys[11].

Child mortality is alarming. Child mortality statistics show the current situation is worse than in the previous decade: child mortality has actually increased to 148 per thousand in 1998 to 126 per thousand in 2001. Child vaccination is still very low in DRC. Less than one child in three receives all the required vaccines. Despite the slight improvement between 2001 and 2007, the level of vaccination is far below 80 percent targeted by the national vaccination program[12].

Maternal health is still a big challenge for the DRC. The DRC is one of the African countries with high fecundity. This situation is the result of weak utilization of modern family planning methods. Male condoms are the most frequent form of contraception utilized in the DRC.

HIV prevalence among pregnant women is around 4.3 percent. Available data prove that higher prevalence rates are found in the east of the country. The systematic recourse to sexual violence by some segments of the population has contributed largely to the spreading of HIV. In the DRC, malaria is still endemic and constitutes the greatest source of morbidity.

---

[11]   Op. cit, p. 30.
[12]   Op. cit. p. 30

High pressure is put on the environment with higher rates in urban than in rural areas [unclear what you mean here]. In fact, 47 percent of the population occupies ten percent of the national territory (source?). As a result, forests disappear quickly around big cities. In Kinshasa, forests have disappeared within a radius of 150 kilometers. Despite its rich endowment, access to potable water in the DRC increased from 22 percent in 2004 to 27 percent in 2005. It is worth mentioning that this rate was 37 percent in 1990, and thus there is still a long run decreasing trend [if I understand you correctly].

In the framework of the world partnership, the DRC enjoys international public aid, which represented 4.48 percent of GDP in 1999. From 2000 to 2005, donors' support was channelled to the government (68 percent) and NGOs (26.4 percent). The DRC has seen the cancellation of $13 billion of its public debt in Highly-Indebted Countries Program (HICP) framework.

There is no sign that the DRC can meet the MDGs without donor support. However, there are no statistics showing clearly the contribution of donors versus the Government. The DRC Government's contribution in establishing an enabling environment, in putting together a reliable database, and coordinating efforts in the various sectors is still paramount.

DRC contribution means strategic thoughts ex-ante to ensure projects implemented countrywide prove enough guarantee for sustainability. This is feasible only through co-funded studies including baseline studies (and subsequent evaluations) aiming at guiding the GDRC's way towards sustainable development.

The achievability of the MDGs depends on the GDRC capacity to manage effectively the inflow of aid that the country is receiving at the national level. Thanks to "groupes thematiques", this work is on good tracks, but work still to be done at the level of every project.

# CHAPTER IV

# BASELINE CONDUCTED AMIDST EASTERN DRC HARDSHIPS

D RC donors' contribution to DRC development will continue to be counterproductive until full coordination is done under the GDRC oversight and leadership. One step towards full coordination is the disclosure of critical studies that may update donors and all stakeholders with current status of development challenges across the country and specifically through well-crafted baseline studies. Below are presented outcomes of the CCC program baseline study deemed a model of baseline studies conducted amidst the presence of various militia groups including may, Rwandese rebels etc.

The key study objectives were to:

1. To provide qualitative and quantitative socio economic data as baseline from which the impacts on human welfare from the JGI—DRC-CCC program can be measured.

2. To test the survey tools and methods in preparation for a more extensive survey of the UGADEC RG in the landscape

## 1. Rationale

In May 2005 Citizens International (CI) undertook a consultancy from the Jane Goodall Institute (JGI), to define and validate indictors for the project performance management plan (PMP). As a result of the consultancy a recommendation was developed to implement a comprehensive baseline survey of indictors for the PMP as well as to collect other more detailed socio-economic data throughout communities in the buffer zones of the community reserves in Landscape 10.

This was not only to provide a baseline by which to assess project impact, but also to provide a more comprehensive picture and quantitative economic understanding of the relationship between people and forests, which might also act as a guide for planning project interventions. It was proposed that the survey be conducted in partnership with the Dian Fossey Gorilla Fund International; this was agreed by both parties in principle. However the cost of implementing such a widespread detailed study was prohibitive in the short term as neither party had budgetary resources of the required magnitude.

JGI began a pilot of their community conservation program in the buffer zone around the Reserve des Gorilles du Tayina (RGT) in 2004 JGI decided that a pilot study should be initiated immediately with available funds, in their pilot program areas, to provide an immediate baseline of data on indicators relevant to the PMP and some of the more detailed economic information. Due to resource constraints the data collected were restricted to quantitative social and economic indices, more detailed qualitative social data through participatory approaches were not collected.

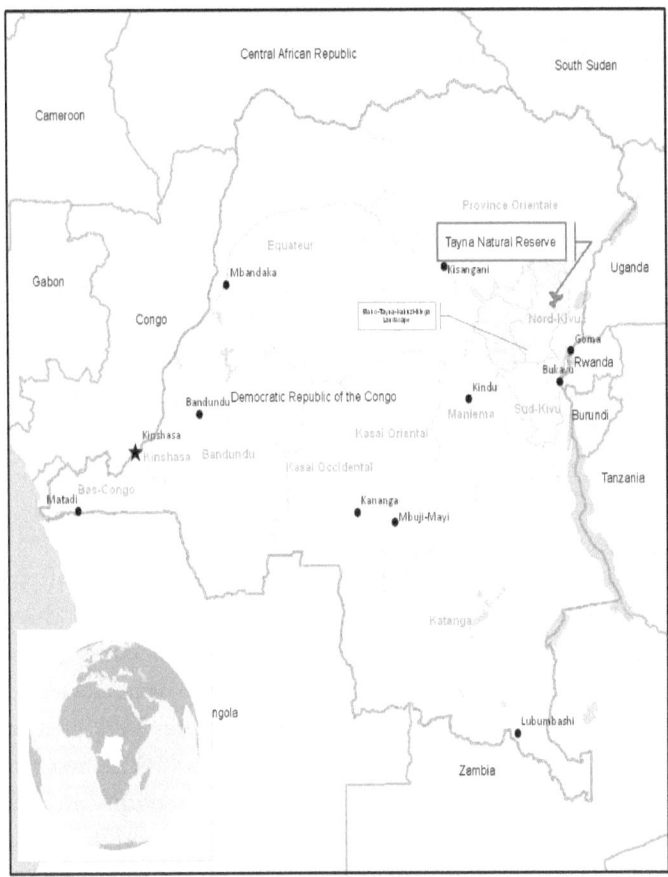

Map 1: Maiko-Tayina-Kahuzi Biega Landscape

## 2. Local forest use and management

Households in the communities surveyed use the natural forest to provide for many household needs, notably fuel wood. With the establishment of the community forest reserve a zoning plan was put in place identifying a core areas for conservation (off limits to any resource exploitation and a buffer zone, within which resource use is allowed. The zoning plan and regulations were agreed upon by community leaders.

Presently there is little enforcement of the zoning plan, with community forest guards, under resourced to effectively implement regulations meant to govern community use of the natural forest. In addition the constant insecurity in the area means that armed militia groups have freedom of access to whatever parts of the forest they wish to hunt or mine minerals; understandably civilian guards are powerless to intervene.

## 3. Structured questionnaire survey

Draft questionnaires were prepared in advance of an enumerator-training workshop held in Lubero over three days (August 25th to 27th)[13]. The method, background theory and questionnaires to be employed were reviewed with enumerators. Some role-playing exercises were used to familiarize the enumerators with the survey tools. A pre test was made on volunteers from the local rural community around the workshop site, to further test for problems with language and comprehension. This allowed enumerators to acquire additional familiarity with the survey tools as well as the chance to apply and review the method. As a result, additional changes were incorporated into the survey questionnaire. These addressed issues to do with enumerator ambiguity or poor comprehension of the questions and to address issues to do with respondent comprehension of questions.

---

[13] Year 2005

A structured survey was used in order to elicit quantitative and qualitative data on household demography, capital assets, household income and expenditure, health, social infrastructure and services and environmental resource use. Whilst a participatory wealth ranking approach was used to identify the community wealth strata for the sample survey, it was not possible to utilize participatory methods to define other qualitative issues to do with forest use and socio-economic conditions. Such techniques could have enabled the study to provide richer data on access and resource use, but given the survey resource constraints and the focus on we decided not to attempt such enquiries. As all the goods reported were traded in the locality, market prices were established by asking respondents to provide price information about goods in the survey.

Once communities were selected (see site selection below), usually a visit was made in advance to alert the relevant authorities to the survey team's arrival and to describe the process. Thus community members were alerted in advance to the possibility of being interviewed. On the day of the survey the team would arrive early in the morning or the evening before. After the wealth ranking exercise was conducted with the village elders, enumerators would then take a local guide to go in search of the randomly selected households. Household interviews were conducted with whoever was present or able to be interviewed in the home at the time (usually the household head or number two with other members present). If an interview was not possible an arrangement was made to return at a more suitable time, or failing that another household was selected at random from the list. Each household was given a gift of salt or other domestic good (value not more then $1US) to thank them for their participation.

## 4. Sources of error and bias

Gathering detailed household accounting data is a challenging task which can be subject to many sources of error. Good data collection relies on well prepared survey tools and thorough training of enumerators. Typically the principal source of error is that of poor respondent recall. It is often difficult to recall exactly how much a household consumes and depending on how long ago the harvest was how much was collected. In general the shorter the recall period is, the more accurate and precise the reporting of income and consumption. Vedeld et al (2004)[14] recommend that it is best practice to make visits once a quarter to a panel of households to build an accurate picture of income and consumption patterns. Whilst repeated visits are technically desirable, panel data collection can also be prohibitively expensive and time consuming, constraints which are applicable to this project. Another source of inaccuracy can come from unusual climatic occurrences such as drought or too much rain, affecting household consumption and production levels. Fortunately the seasons prior and during our data collection were not considered unusual.

Unfortunately human bias can also cause significant error in the data; this can come both from enumerators and respondents. A key source of enumerator bias can be the use of questions that lead to a particular answer i.e. questions are phrased to elicit a certain type of response. To control for enumerator bias, the survey questionnaire was rigorously screened in order to make the language as neutral as possible and avoid leading questions In addition enumerators went

---

[14]    Bush Glenn and Mumbere Muhongya Olivier: '*Baseline Study Report for the CCC Project*', 2005

through a training program to clearly explain and test how they went about administering the survey. Respondent bias is more difficult to control for. Either a respondent may wish to conceal information i.e. about illegal activities, or for income tax purposes, or misinform in the expectation of being able to receive benefits from rural development projects. Importantly respondents were ensured complete anonymity and no data that could identify the household was collected (names, exact locations etc.)

To further control for bias a clear explanation of the purpose and objective of the survey was delivered to each household before the interview. In addition discrete observations were made by enumerators of each household's situation on approaching the home. If enumerators clearly saw discrepancies between what was reported and what could be observed then polite but probing questions were made to elicit a realistic response i.e. if hunting apparatus was evident in the home and the respondent did not acknowledge hunting in the forest, the enumerator politely asked who the hunting equipment actually belonged to.

More difficult to control for is respondent deliberately giving misleading answers in the hope of some beneficial outcome for the household or community. For example if a new development or poverty alleviation project is expected to come to the area, community members may under report their income levels in order to create a picture far worse than reality to ensure that project activities come to their area and not a neighboring one. However observations on the ground clearly point to a low level of physical and human development in all communities, thus we are confident that the data are truly representative of local conditions.

However we feel that the data under estimates household income and consumption, because of poor recall and omissions, but it is difficult to know by how much. However we feel that any underestimation is probably evenly spread across all the household income data collected therefore there will be little effect on the trends and patterns observed.

## 5. Understanding wealth in socio-economic analysis

A useful approach to the analysis of how forests contribute to livelihoods is through the analysis of the importance of forests to different wealth groups. This focus can be useful in that understanding the proportionate role and nature of forest resources in livelihoods strategies i.e. to help target precise interventions to different groups of people.

The sampling was therefore structured to ensure three different wealth groups were surveyed (poor, average wealth and relatively rich) in each village community.

Wealth should be considered a composite measure of not only income, but the value of other household assets. However due to the low ownership of assets in this context, income alone is a sufficient proxy measure of wealth. Therefore in this study where we refer to income this may also imply wealth, but where we refer to wealth we do not necessarily imply income alone. The measure of income used in this study comprises goods sold, the prevailing market value of own-produced goods consumed in the home, monetary and, non-monetary transfers into the household account, and income from wage labor in cash or the value of goods in kind.

Wealth can be considered a relative concept depending on unit of analysis. A household that earns $1000 per annum and has 5 members is perhaps more wealthy on a per capita basis than a household that earns $1000 and has 10 members. However, a larger household enjoys better economies of scale than smaller households with more labor available for different activities. In addition the composition of a household in terms of age and sex structure affects levels of production and consumption of the household as a unit of analysis (Campbell & Luckert, 2002; Deaton, 1998). In order to make valid comparisons in absolute terms across households an "adjusted net household income" was therefore used in this study, to reduce bias in inter-household comparisons of wealth.

Adjusted net income was calculated by dividing the total net income by a factor comprised of two coefficients of adult equivalency and economy of scale, to give an adjusted equivalent unit (AEU) derived from World Health Organization methodology reported in Campbell & Luckert, 2002[15]. A household's AEU was calculated according to the following procedure. A coefficient of a standard adult equivalent unit is awarded to each household member. The sum of the coefficients gives a standardised measure of household size. Each household was scored on its number of occupants and given a coefficient of economy of scale.

---

[15]   Bush Glenn and Mumbere Muhongya Olivier; Idem.

**Table 1.01 Coefficients for adult equivalence and household economies for scale calculations (Adapted from Campbell and Luckert 2002)**

| Adult equivalent scale | | | Household economy scale | |
|---|---|---|---|---|
| Age | Male | Female | Household Size | Economy of scale |
| 0-2 | | 0.40 | 1-2 | 1.000 |
| 3-4 | | 0.48 | 3 | 0.946 |
| 5-6 | | 0.56 | 4 | 0.897 |
| 7-8 | | 0.64 | 5 | 0.851 |
| 9-10 | | 0.76 | 6 | 0.807 |
| 11-12 | 0.80 | 0.88 | 7 | 0.778 |
| 13-14 | 1.00 | 1.00 | 8 | 0.757 |
| 15-18 | 1.20 | 1.00 | 9 | 0.741 |
| 19-59 | 1.00 | 0.88 | 10 | 0.729 |
| 60+ | 0.88 | 0.72 | 10+ | 0.719 |

The absolute income (net value) is then divided by the two coefficients to give the AEU (referred to as an *adjusted* value). This helps to account for biases other wise introduced if comparisons are made on the basis of unadjusted income. Effectively the adjusted income value gives a figure that depicts household income on the basis of a standard adult unit. Therefore in the results section inter household comparisons analysis of income and consumption are conducted using income quartiles based on the adjusted total income figures.

It is important to be aware that all of the households interviewed in this study are poor or ultra poor in global development terms. Wealth groups (poor, average and wealthy) are used in a relative context in this study to differentiate between different groups in the context of a single community. Subsequent comparisons on the basis of wealth or income are carried out using income quartiles, not the wealth categories.

## 6. Survey sites and sampling

The suggested pilot survey area is the communities in the development zone of the Tayina RGT. At the community level a number of strata have been identified. Both large 300 plus households and smaller villages up to 300 households have been identified. These exist in zones with both good (a dirt road) and poor access (by foot to a dirt road) to large markets.

A purposive sample was conducted of communities, represented by Kasugho, Fatoua and Mbuhi (Table 1.01)

Table 1.02 Description of villages

| Village Name | Number of respondents | Approximate number of households | Distance from Butembo (km) (Approximate distance by easiest overland route) |
|---|---|---|---|
| Kasugho | 30 | 350 | 100 |
| Mbuhi | 30 | 72 | 125 |
| Fatoua | 30 | 102 | 150 |

A key assumption was that various income groups used the forest resources in different ways and displayed varying levels of forest use to maintain their livelihood.

Wealth groups were identified in each community in a participatory wealth ranking exercise with community leaders. The wealth ranking exercise involved a discussion of wealth issues and the local indicators of wealth and the establishment of a set of indicators for three wealth categories (poor average and wealthy). The elders were then asked to distribute households amongst the wealth categories.

At the household level a random sample survey of households, stratified according to wealth categories of high, middle and low income. 10 households were sampled from each wealth category. Households were then assigned a number within each stratum then 10 families from each group chosen at random. A total of 90 households (30 from each village) in the three communities were interviewed.

## 7. Key Findings

### 7.1. Community and Household Demography

Table 2.1 shows the number of males and females in respondent households as well as the proportion of females. Across all sites and for each community the ratio of males to females was roughly equal.

**Table 2.01 Number of males and females and proportion of females in respondent households**

| Village | Count of Females in respondent household | Count of Males | Combined | %Female |
|---------|------------------------------------------|----------------|----------|---------|
| Fatoua | 106 | 103 | 209 | 50.72 |
| Kasugho | 106 | 91 | 197 | 53.81 |
| Mbuhi | 99 | 102 | 201 | 49.25 |
| All | 311 | 296 | 607 | 51.24 |

In addition there was no significant difference between men and women in terms of the mean age of household occupants

**Table 2.02 Average age by gender (years)**

| Village | Female | Male | Combined |
|---------|--------|------|----------|
| Fatoua | 22.3 | 20.1 | 21.2 |
| Kasugho | 21.8 | 23.3 | 22.6 |
| Mbuhi | 21.8 | 21.4 | 21.7 |
| All | 22 | 21.6 | 21.8 |

The overall average household occupancy was 6.7 individuals (adults and children combined) and no significant difference was found between communities.

Across all communities a large proportion of households had been resident for 10 years or more (Table 2.3). However a significant number of households had only been resident for less than ten years, with a notable number of households having migrated to the communities between 1 and 5 years ago.

**Table 2.03 Time spent in location (% of households by category)**

| Village | Less than 1 year | Between 1 and 5 years | Between 5 and 10 years | 10 years or more |
|---------|-----------|----------|----------|----------|
| Fatoua | 10.00 | 3.33 | 13.33 | 73.33 |
| Kasugho | 0.00 | 30.00 | 3.33 | 66.67 |
| Mbuhi | 13.33 | 13.33 | 0.00 | 73.33 |
| All | 7.78 | 15.56 | 5.56 | 71.11 |

Thus the communities may be characterised as growing, with a large proportion of that growth coming from people migrating into the communities from elsewhere such as neighbouring communities or from further away. Anecdotal evidence points towards economic reasons for the influx of people, with either the prospect of land for cultivation out of former natural forests or due to being displaced from other areas due to civil war.

## 7.2. Age Sex Distribution

Table 2.4 shows the population distribution between sexes amongst different age ranges. Over all there is no significant difference in the distribution, but within the 21 to 30, and 31 to 40 categories there is a difference in the ration of females to males. The data shows that there are a higher proportion of women to men overall communities and within each community.

**Table 2.04 Proportion of males and females in different age categories**

| | | Combined | | FATOUA | | KASUGHO | | MBUHI | |
|---|---|---|---|---|---|---|---|---|---|
| Group | Age Range | % Male | % Female | % Male | % Female | % Male | % Female | % Male | % Female |
| 1 | 0 to 10 | 16.47 | 15.16 | 18.66 | 14.83 | 11.68 | 15.23 | 18.91 | 15.42 |
| 2 | 11 to 20 | 15.65 | 15.32 | 15.79 | 15.79 | 17.26 | 16.75 | 13.93 | 13.43 |
| 3 | 21 to 30 | 4.61 | 8.73 | 3.35 | 5.74 | 5.08 | 10.15 | 5.47 | 10.45 |
| 4 | 31 to 40 | 3.79 | 5.77 | 4.31 | 9.09 | 2.54 | 3.05 | 4.48 | 4.98 |
| 5 | 41 to 50 | 3.29 | 3.29 | 3.35 | 2.87 | 4.06 | 5.08 | 2.49 | 1.99 |
| 6 | 51 to 60 | 2.80 | 1.65 | 1.91 | 1.44 | 3.55 | 2.54 | 2.99 | 1.00 |
| 7 | 60 + | 2.14 | 1.32 | 1.91 | 0.96 | 2.03 | 1.02 | 2.49 | 1.99 |

The RGT region has experienced a high level of insecurity from civil war and insurgencies over the past decade. It could be that there are fewer men in age groups 3 and 4 as a result of this, as males from these categories may be considered to be prime candidates to make up the ranks of various militia groups, or be targeted as the victims of civil unrest. This aspect needs to be clarified. Importantly this points towards a potential lack of human resources to undertake key tasks such as heavy manual labour in the household. Other factors that may explain the lower number of males are; men often migrate to find labour and may not return; men are more likely to contract HIV and die from AIDS because of their higher mobility throughout the region.

## 7.3. Education

The level of education and whether individuals were still at school was determined for household members. Table 2.5 shows that only 26.4% of household members of school age had not received or were not currently receiving some form of education. Over all communities 59.4% had or were currently receiving a primary education. However, the number of people receiving secondary or tertiary education declined sharply to 14.4% and 0.8% respectively.

**Table 2.05 Education level (% of household individuals by level)**

| Village | No Formal | Primary | Secondary | Tertiary |
|---------|-----------|---------|-----------|----------|
| Fatoua | 24.64 | 64.93 | 10.43 | 0.00 |
| Kasugho | 16.26 | 55.83 | 26.83 | 1.08 |
| Mbuhi | 41.26 | 56.64 | 2.10 | 0.00 |
| All | 26.40 | 59.40 | 14.40 | 0.80 |

Table 2.6 shows the proportion of men and women receiving formal education. Across tabulation analysis of the differences in education levels between men and women showed that over all communities women were less likely to receive formal education than men and were also much less likely to go on to secondary and tertiary education, although there was no significant difference in the likelihood of receiving primary education (ChiSq=10.135, d.f. =3, $p<0.05$).

**Table 2.06 Education level by gender (% of household individuals by education level)**

| Village | No Formal | | Primary | | Secondary | | Tertiary | |
|---|---|---|---|---|---|---|---|---|
| | Female | Male | Female | Male | Female | Male | Female | Male |
| Fatoua | 28.48 | 21.11 | 71.52 | 58.89 | 0.00 | 20.00 | 0.00 | 0.00 |
| Kasugho | 17.62 | 14.77 | 59.07 | 52.27 | 23.32 | 30.68 | 0.00 | 2.27 |
| Mbuhi | 51.91 | 32.26 | 45.80 | 65.81 | 2.29 | 1.94 | 0.00 | 0.00 |
| All | 30.47 | 22.50 | 59.71 | 59.10 | 9.82 | 18.79 | 0.00 | 1.57 |

## 7.4. Employment

An assessment of the different types of employment of household members was conducted (table 2.7). Overall communities' salaried employment amongst adults was very low 3.2% of the population, with the majority of household members falling in to the subsistence agriculture category 39.9% of household members. Of the minors, the majority were students or children, pre school age.

**Table 2.07 Employment (% of adult household members)**

| Village | No employment | Subsistence agriculture | Student | Trader | Unsalaried worker | Salaried worker | Child | Other |
|---|---|---|---|---|---|---|---|---|
| Fatoua | 2.61 | 42.90 | 37.68 | 0.87 | 0.00 | 1.74 | 13.62 | 0.58 |
| Kasugho | 0.81 | 36.04 | 42.01 | 2.71 | 0.81 | 4.88 | 9.76 | 2.98 |
| Mbuhi | 0.70 | 41.26 | 34.27 | 0.70 | 0.35 | 2.80 | 19.58 | 0.35 |
| All | 1.40 | 39.90 | 38.30 | 1.50 | 0.40 | 3.20 | 13.90 | 1.40 |

An analysis of the differences in employment rates between men and women in selected employment categories Table 2.8) shows that women were more likely to be unemployed, were less employed in subsistence agriculture than men and were more likely to obtain salaried employment than men. A contingency table analysis showed the differences in employment figures between men and women to be significant (ChiSq=16.096, d.f.=7, p<0.05).

Table 2.08 Employment in selected categories by gender

| Village | No employment | | Subsistence agriculture | | Salaried worker | |
|---|---|---|---|---|---|---|
| | Male | Female | Male | Female | Male | Female |
| Fatoua | 1.82 | 3.33 | 51.52 | 35.00 | 0.00 | 3.33 |
| Kasugho | 0.00 | 1.70 | 41.45 | 30.11 | 6.22 | 3.41 |
| Mbuhi | 0.76 | 0.65 | 47.33 | 36.13 | 0.00 | 5.16 |
| All | 0.82 | 1.96 | 46.42 | 33.66 | 2.45 | 3.91 |

## 7.5. Materials Assets

## 7.5.1. Housing

Table 3.01 and 3.02 show the proportions of households with homes made from a selection of materials. The majority of houses were constructed from wattle and daub (thin sticks woven through the house frame and mud plaster) and thatched roofs. The plastic sheeting mentioned was predominantly UNHCR white sheeting commonly found throughout the region. It is not clear whether or not households had purchased the sheeting, or received it as emergency aid from relief organisations.

Table 3.01 Wall construction (% of households by material)

| Village | Timber | Mud | Wattle and daub |
|---|---|---|---|
| FATOUA | 20.00 | 0.00 | 80.00 |
| KASUGHO | 6.67 | 0.00 | 93.33 |
| MBUHI | 16.67 | 6.67 | 76.67 |
| ALL | 14.44 | 2.22 | 83.33 |

**Table 3.02 Roof Construction (% of households by material)**

| Village | Thatch | Iron Sheets | Plastic Sheeting |
|---------|--------|-------------|------------------|
| FATOUA | 83.33 | 6.67 | 10.00 |
| KASUGHO | 66.67 | 33.33 | 0.00 |
| MBUHI | 100.00 | 0.00 | 0.00 |
| ALL | 83.33 | 13.33 | 3.33 |

Possession of other material assets was also very low. Table 3.03 shows the number of selected material assets per household. Although radio ownership was moderate (about 45%) possession of material assets that might make a contribution t improved household welfare such as bicycles for transport was very low.

**Table 3.03 Ownership of other assets (average items per. Household)**

| Village | Bicycle | Radio | Television | Motorcycle | Car |
|---------|---------|-------|------------|------------|-----|
| FATOUA | 0.03 | 0.47 | 0.00 | 0.00 | 0.00 |
| KASUGHO | 0.17 | 0.53 | 0.00 | 0.03 | 0.00 |
| MBUHI | 0.00 | 0.33 | 0.00 | 0.00 | 0.00 |
| ALL | 0.07 | 0.44 | 0.00 | 0.01 | 0.00 |

As this is a region of high insecurity both currently and for the last decade, the need for families to periodically flee their homes may mean that certain items may have had to be left behind and subject to looting. Only small items such as radios may be easily transported to safety. Similarly houses left behind may have been ransacked for valuable building materials or raised to the ground during fighting.

However one of the key constraint identified during the selection of the survey communities was varying degrees of market access due to increasingly poor communications i.e. Kasugho, closest to Lubero/Butembo and Fatoua furthest away, none of them having a road accessible to vehicles open throughout the year and Mbuhi only accessible on foot along small forest paths. Improving market access through appropriate transportation mechanisms could have a profound impact on the livelihoods of households.

### 7.5.2. Livestock

Livestock owner ship (Table 3.04) was very low on the whole; particularly larger ruminants such as cows, goats and sheep were poorly represented. Household averages numbers for poultry was the highest followed by guinea pigs.

**Table 3.04 Livestock Ownership (Average per household)**

| Village | GOATS | SHEEP | PIGS | POULTRY | RABBITS | GUINEA PIGS | COWS |
|---|---|---|---|---|---|---|---|
| FATOUA | 0.00 | 0.00 | 0.00 | 2.67 | 0.00 | 0.63 | 0.00 |
| KASUGHO | 1.00 | 0.33 | 0.23 | 2.14 | 0.03 | 5.43 | 0.40 |
| MBUHI | 0.07 | 0.00 | 0.13 | 1.80 | 0.00 | 0.43 | 0.00 |
| ALL | 0.36 | 0.11 | 0.12 | 2.20 | 0.01 | 2.17 | 0.13 |

The proportion of households not owning any livestock at all (Table 3.05) was 27.78% over all villages. There was also a significant difference in the number of households without livestock between villages. (Chi Sq 17.516, d.f. = 2, $p<0.01$)

**Table 3.05 Livestock Ownership**

| Village | % of households with no livestock |
|---|---|
| FATOUA | 30.00 |
| KASUGHO | 10.00 |
| MBUHI | 43.33 |
| ALL | 27.78 |

### 7.5.3. Land

Analysis of land holdings (table 3.06) showed the average holdings per household for each village and overall. Households in Fatoua had higher arable land holdings than Kasugho or Mbuhi and also had significantly higher areas of plantation (cash crops) and kitchen gardens and woodlots.

**Table 3.06 Land holdings by type (Average area Ha.)**

| Village | Natural Forest | Woodlot | Arable | Plantation | Kitchen Garden |
|---------|----------------|---------|--------|------------|----------------|
| FATOUA | 3.31 | 2.82 | 4.97 | 0.64 | 0.49 |
| KASUGHO | 5.86 | 0.89 | 1.88 | 0.34 | 0.00 |
| MBUHI | 1.89 | 1.07 | 2.28 | 0.00 | 0.07 |
| ALL | 3.69 | 1.60 | 3.04 | 0.33 | 0.19 |

Mbuhi had the lowest average holdings of woodlots, despite having the least access to areas of natural forest; additionally amongst Mbuhi households no cash crop production was recorded. Anecdotal evidence suggests woodlots are primarily used for building materials (poles) rather than for domestic fuel wood.

Some pasture areas were recorded, but they were few, with households tending to rough graze their animals, including allowing them to forage in natural forest areas.

Kasugho no Kitchen gardens were recorded, this is possibly as a result of Kasugho being a more urbanised than the other villages, i.e. having less space around the houses, or preferring to leave agricultural activities to the fields surrounding the villages.

### 7.5.4. Association Membership

On average 34.4% of households (Table 3.07) belonged to some form of association involved in rural development activities. These associations predominantly gave assistance with advice on health and agricultural development issues, but anecdotal evidence indicated that little material assistance was obtained, and in fact that many of the associations were not fully operational.

## Table 3.07 Membership of an association

| Village | % households in an association |
|---|---|
| FATOUA | 26.6 |
| KASUGHO | 60 |
| MBUHI | 16.6 |
| All | 34.4 |

**ASSOCIATIONS Named**

| Village | | | | | | | | |
|---|---|---|---|---|---|---|---|---|
| FATOUA | CBCE | CBCA | JEUNESSE | | | | | |
| KASUGHO | ACOGENOKI | ACOPLKA | APETAMACO | CACUDEKI | CARITAS | CEPROSAM | FEC | FRATERNITE | GARD |
| MBUHI | CBCE | CSMBUHI | ORPALU | | | | | |

A full list of association acronyms and what their major activities are can be found in Appendix 2.

### 7.5.5. Credit

Overall credit access was very poor (table 3.08), with only just over 11% of households indicating that they knew of credit sources that they might be eligible for.

**Table 3.08 Credit Access**

| Village | % with credit access |
|---------|----------------------|
| FATOUA | 16.67 |
| KASUGHO | 6.67 |
| MBUHI | 16.67 |
| ALL | 13.33 |

There were few organisations named as providing sources of credit (Table 3.09). Having access to cash to purchase inputs into agriculture or other business ventures is a key bottle neck to development activities. None the less the few sources available are very important. From a development program perspective it would be interesting to see if synergies between the named organisations and the CCC program could be developed to assist in promoting rural credit activities.

**Table 3.09 Number of households using credit from different sources**

| Village | CBCA | EGL CATH | EGLISE | F ET FAM | MUT LOC |
|---------|------|----------|--------|----------|---------|
| FATOUA | 3 | | | 1 | |
| KASUGHO | | | 1 | | |
| MBUHI | | 1 | 2 | | 1 |
| All | 3 | 1 | 3 | 1 | 1 |

Despite 13% of households indicating that credit sources were available, just over 11% of households actually used the credit sources (Table 3.10).

**Table 3.10 % Households using credit**

| Village | Yes | No | % credit use |
|---------|-----|-----|--------------|
| FATOUA | 4 | 26 | 15.38 |
| KASUGHO | 1 | 29 | 3.45 |
| MBUHI | 4 | 26 | 15.39 |
| All | 9 | 81 | 11.11 |

Interestingly over all villages there was no correlation between income (as an indicator of wealth), education level of the household and credit use. However households in Kasugho seemed to have much worse access to credit than household sin either Fatoua or Mbuhi.

## 7.6. Environmental resource Use

### 7.6.1. Woody biomass

Table 4.01 shows the average time to walk one way to the natural forest from each community. Over all villages the average time spent to walk one way to the nearest natural forest was just under half an hour (0.45 of an hour).

**Table 4.01 Average Time to get to forest (one way)**

| Village | Av Time (Decimal hours) |
|---------|--------------------------|
| FATOUA | 0.55 |
| KASUGHO | 1.00 |
| MBUHI | 0.30 |
| All | 0.45 |

100% of households interviewed were dependant on woody biomass for domestic use. Table 4.02 shows average household consumption of fuel wood per week. The units used are bundles, effectively a head load (the weight of wood that a person may carry comfortably on their head. There was a significant difference in the wood consumed between villages, with households in Fatoua consuming less than those in Kasugho or Mbuhi (Anova, F= 3.726, d.f. = 2, p<0.05).

**Table 4.02 Domestic Fuel Wood Use**

| Village | Average number of bundles |
|---------|---------------------------|
| FATOUA | 3.33 |
| KASUGHO | 4.33 |
| MBUHI | 4.1 |
| All | 3.9 |

Interestingly there is no significant difference in household size between communities, this result may be inaccurate because the amount of wood that may be carried per head load may vary greatly depending on the physique of the person and who in the household is allocated the task of collecting fuel wood i.e. children may not carry as much as an adult.

Across all villages charcoal use was low, Table 4.03 shows that on average 88.89% of households do not use charcoal. Presumably this is because the close proximity of natural forests means using fuel wood is still an easy alternative form a logistical point of view.

**Table 4.03 Charcoal use**

| Village | % not using |
|---------|-------------|
| FATOUA | 100.00 |
| KASUGHO | 73.33 |
| MBUHI | 93.33 |
| All | 88.89 |

More qualitative research may reveal the social reason behind wood vs. charcoal use, as well as other aspects of the use of wood in the domestic environment.

### 7.6.2. Domestic Water

Collecting water is an important daily task in the household and on average about one hour per day is spent by household members collecting sufficient water for domestic purposes Table 4.05).

**Table 4.04 Average time spent Collecting water**

| Village | hours |
|---------|-------|
| FATOUA | 1.00 |
| KASUGHO | 1.10 |
| MBUHI | 1.00 |
| All | 1.04 |

Households reported that the majority of their domestic water was supplied from surface water sources (Table 4.04) these being both streams and rivers or protected and unprotected springs. A protected spring is one where some form of civil works have been performed to allow the spring water to collect in a well or sump for ease of collection (sometimes with a spigot) and to minimise the disturbance to water emanating from the mouth of the spring itself.

**Table 4.05 Main Water (proportion % of households)**

| Village | Bore hole | Stream /River | Protected Spring | Unprotected Spring |
|---|---|---|---|---|
| FATOUA | 0.00 | 63.33 | 0.00 | 36.67 |
| KASUGHO | 0.00 | 3.33 | 70.00 | 26.67 |
| MBUHI | 3.33 | 56.67 | 0.00 | 40.00 |
| All | 1.11 | 41.11 | 23.33 | 34.44 |

From a human health perspective water from boreholes and protected springs should have lower levels of sediment than from other categories. A large proportion if the population only had access to unprotected springs or stream sand rivers as their principle source of domestic water.

Table 4.06 shows the number of households treating drinking water before consumption. Only 4.4% of households across all villages treated their drinking water by boiling. Boiling was the only type of treatment recorded in all villages. Again from a human health perspective this leaves people very vulnerable to a host of enteric diseases that would otherwise be easily preventable simply through boiling drinking water. However boiling water requires fuel wood and this activity can also have a negative impact on natural forest resources as harvesting rates of fuel wood may increase. Thus any initiative requiring increased amounts of domestic fuel needs to mitigate the problems fro the outset i.e. by introducing fuel efficient stoves, or encouraging tree planting for fuel wood.

**Table 4.06 Water Treatment**

| Village | % treating water by boiling |
|---|---|
| FATOUA | 6.7 |
| KASUGHO | 3.3 |
| MBUHI | 3.396.67 |
| All | 4.4 |

Additionally there are potential labour constraints, and more qualitative research needs to be carried out to understand the division of household labour and activity budgets. A clearer understanding of the time and labour costs and benefits of introducing new technologies is needed in order to understand how their adoption might be affected by human resource constraints in the home.

Some questions were asked regarding the quality of drinking water (able 4.07) and how this may have changed over time (Table 4.08). Across all villages the average proportion of households indicating that their water source was clear without any sediment was just over 71%. However between villages there was a significant different in peoples perceptions, with only 66.67% in Mbuhi and only 50% in Fatoua saying their water was clear (Chi Sq= 16.334, d.f. = 2, p<0.01).

**Table 4.07 Quality assessment**

| Village | Clear | Some sediment | %of people indicating their water is clear |
|---------|-------|---------------|---------------------------------------------|
| FATOUA | 15 | 15 | 50.00 |
| KASUGHO | 29 | 1 | 96.67 |
| MBUHI | 20 | 10 | 66.67 |
| All | 64 | 26 | 71.11 |

**Table 4.08 Change In quality last five years (% of households)**

| Village | Improved | No change | Worse |
|---------|----------|-----------|-------|
| FATOUA | 3.33 | 96.67 | 0.00 |
| KASUGHO | 20.00 | 76.67 | 3.33 |
| MBUHI | 0.00 | 100.00 | 0.00 |
| **All** | **7.78** | **91.11** | **1.11** |

During the last five years most households (91.11%) felt that there had been no change in water quality. Clearly in terms of human development and social impact much could be achieved through basic health education about water treatment and investment in access to improved water sources.

### 7.6.3. Medicinal Plants

Medicinal plant use in the survey communities was high, with only 16.67% of respondents never using them.

**Table 4.09 Medicinal Plant Use**

| Village | YES | NO | Grand Total | % not using |
|---------|-----|-----|-------------|-------------|
| FATOUA | 26 | 4 | 30 | 13.33 |
| KASUGHO | 21 | 9 | 30 | 30.00 |
| MBUHI | 28 | 2 | 30 | 6.67 |
| ALL | 75 | 15 | 90 | 16.67 |

The main use of medicinal plants was in the treatment of fever associated with a number of different problems.

**Table 4.10 Main uses of medicinal plants**
**(% of those who actually use)**

| Village | Malaria | Fever | Enteric problems |
|---------|---------|-------|------------------|
| FATOUA | 2.67 | 92.00 | 5.33 |
| KASUGHO | 3.39 | 96.61 | 0.00 |
| MBUHI | 0.06 | 0.58 | 0.36 |
| ALL | 4.25 | 80.66 | 15.09 |

## 7.7. Sanitation and Health Care

### 7.7.1. Latrines

Disposal of human waste is an issue of great concern in Fatoua and Mbuhi. Table 5.01 shows that 23.3% and 40% of respondents did not have access to a pit latrine. These values are significantly different from Kasugho (Chi. Sq = 9.137, d.f. = 2, p<0.01)

**Table 5.01 Access to Pit Latrine**

| Village | % without access |
|---------|------------------|
| FATOUA | 23.33 |
| KASUGHO | 6.67 |
| MBUHI | 40.00 |
| **All** | **23.33** |

Education people about the need for and use of pit latrines could have significant impact on the prevalence of enteric diseases in these communities. Of course there may be labour constraints or other factors that prevent households from digging pit latrines, and these issues must be clarified through more detailed research on labour resources

### 7.7.2. Clinics

In all communities there was reasonable access to clinics, However in Mbuhi 20% of the population indicated that they did not have access.

**Table 5.02 Access to Clinic**

| Village | YES | NO | Grand Total | %without access |
|---------|-----|-----|------------|-----------------|
| FATOUA | 29 | 1 | 30 | 3.33 |
| KASUGHO | 29 | 1 | 30 | 3.33 |
| MBUHI | 24 | 6 | 30 | 20.00 |
| All | 82 | 8 | 90 | 8.89 |

On further inspection lack of access to a clinic may be related to the travel times (Table 5.03). It can be clearly seen that average travel time for a household to a clinic in Mbuhi village is significantly higher at over six hours compared to Fatoua and Kasugho (ANOVA, F=330.769, d.f. = 2, p<0.001)

**Table 5.03 Average travel time (one way) to the clinic**

| Village | Time hours |
|---------|-----------|
| FATOUA | 0.67 |
| KASUGHO | 1.00 |
| MBUHI | 6.37 |
| ALL | 5.44 |

Clearly having health services at hand is an important first step in addressing health issues, and is clearly a priority issue in Mbuhi. However Mbuhi village is not a geographically tight community, in that the village is spread widely over the land on which people cultivate, unlike Kasugho and Fatoua, where there is a clearly defined centralised conglomeration of households, with people going out from the village to their fields.

### 7.7.3. Health Fund

All respondents in the survey indicated that they knew of a health fund that could assist in developing their means of paying for health care. However accessing the fund was a different matter (Table 5.04), in that only one respondent in Fatoua indicated that they were able to take part in the fund. Incidentally that household were in the upper end of the top income quartile i.e. one of the wealthiest household in the data set.

**Table 5.04 Using fund**

| Village | % using fund |
|---------|--------------|
| FATOUA | 3.33 |
| KASUGHO | 0 |
| MBUHI | 0 |
| ALL | 1.11 |

Therefore for the majority of households paying for health care is a problem.

### 7.7.4. Vaccinations

A high proportion of households reported that they had received vaccinations of one sort of another (Table 5.05). In all villages, only 5.56% of respondents reported that they had not received vaccinations that year.

**Table 5.05 Households receiving vaccinations**

| Village | %not receiving vaccinations |
|---------|------------------------------|
| FATOUA | 6.67 |
| KASUGHO | 0.00 |
| MBUHI | 10.00 |
| ALL | 5.56 |

Across all villages, about 95% of households interviewed reported that they had received vaccinations against Polio, Typhoid, meningitis, measles and BCG (Table 5.06).

**Table 5.06 Vaccinations received by type (% households)**

|         | POLIO  | TYPHOID | MENINGITIS | MEASELS | BCG    |
|---------|--------|---------|------------|---------|--------|
| VILLAGE | YES    | YES     | YES        | YES     | YES    |
| FATOUA  | 93.33  | 3.33    | 3.33       | 93.33   | 93.33  |
| KASUGHO | 100.00 | 0.00    | 0.00       | 100.00  | 100.00 |
| MBUHI   | 93.33  | 0.00    | 0.00       | 90.00   | 93.33  |
| ALL     | 95.56  | 1.11    | 1.11       | 94.44   | 95.56  |

Households in Mbuhi and Fatoua did report not receiving one or other of the vaccinations. Although there was a 100% response for meningitis, and Typhoid in Mbuhi for other categories of vaccination and across all categories in Fatoua, there were some negative responses. Negative responses could have occurred because individuals may not have been sure which vaccinations they had actually received, or simply because of poor access to the clinics to get vaccinations, may not have bothered.

### 7.8. Family Planning Reproductive Health

### 7.8.1. Family Planning

Interestingly overall villages there was a 75% response that households had received some advice on family planning matters (table 6.01).

Table 6.01 Household access to family planning advice

| Village | YES | NO | Grand Total | % no advice |
|---|---|---|---|---|
| FATOUA | 22 | 8 | 30 | 73.33 |
| KASUGHO | 22 | 8 | 30 | 73.33 |
| MBUHI | 24 | 6 | 30 | 80.00 |
| ALL | 68 | 22 | 90 | 75.56 |

Noticeably in all communities (Table 6.02) the local clinic/ health post played a prominent role in delivering family planning advice. In addition contact with the church and listening to the radio made up the next most listened to sources of advice.

Table 6.02 Sources of family planning advice

| Village | ADBC | CBCA | CBCE | EGLISE | POST SANTE | Post Sante | RADIO | RGT | VOYAGES |
|---|---|---|---|---|---|---|---|---|---|
| FATOUA | | 2 | | 2 | 1 | 15 | | | 1 |
| KASUGHO | 3 | | | 1 | | 12 | 6 | | |
| MBUHI | | 1 | 1 | 4 | . | 18 | | 1 | |
| ALL | 3 | 3 | 1 | 7 | 1 | 45 | 6 | 1 | 1 |

### 7.8.2. Contraception

The most popular form of contraception (Table 6.03) over all villages was the natural rhythm method[16] (37.78%) followed by condoms (5.56%)

---

[16] Natural contraception, is also known as the rhythm method, where the number of days since a woman's most fertile period are counted to know the days when sexual intercourse are least likely to result in pregnancy. This is sometimes known as the necklace method, where women use a necklace of different coloured beads to count the days as they go by, the days on which there is a high risk of pregnancy are denoted by a brightly coloured bead.

**Table 6.03 Contraceptive use by type (% households)**

| Village | Condom | Oral Contraceptives | Natural | Mix (condom and natural) |
|---|---|---|---|---|
| | yes | yes | yes | no |
| FATOUA | 6.67 | 0.00 | 50.00 | 93.33 |
| KASUGHO | 10.00 | 3.33 | 30.00 | 90.00 |
| MBUHI | 0.00 | 0.00 | 33.33 | 100.00 |
| ALL | 5.56 | 1.11 | 37.78 | 94.44 |

Actual use of contraceptive methods for family planning was low, fifty four out of the ninety households interviewed used no form of contraception at all, a rate of 60%. This was despite 75% of all houses having reported some knowledge of family planning issues. The key sources of contraceptives (Table 6.04) or necklaces (see footnote 1) were mainly from expert persons i.e. project representatives, or from the local health post and the church.

**Table 6.04 Reported sources of contraceptives**

| Village | ADBC | AMIS | CBCA | EGLISE | EXP PERS. | PS | RCT |
|---|---|---|---|---|---|---|---|
| FATOUA | | 1 | 1 | 2 | 6 | 4 | |
| KASUGHO | 1 | | | 1 | 7 | 1 | 1 |
| MBUHI | | | | 1 | 6 | 1 | |
| ALL | 1 | 1 | 1 | 4 | 19 | 6 | 1 |

In terms of reasons why contraception should be used fifty out of ninety (55.6%) respondents said it was to reduce the risk of contracting sexually transmitted diseases i.e. condoms, but condom use was reported in less than 4% of households. More research Is needed on the availability and also the acceptability of different contraception methods.

### 7.8.3. Prenatal Health

Over all villages just over 72 % of households reported that they had some received to pre natal healthcare or advice (Table 6.05)

**Table 6.05 Access to prenatal health advice**

| Village | % without advice |
|---------|------------------|
| FATOUA | 86.67 |
| KASUGHO | 76.67 |
| MBUHI | 53.33 |
| **ALL** | **72.22** |

The only source of prenatal advice reported was from the local health post (Table 6.06)

**Table 6.06 Main source of pre-natal advice**

| Village | None | Post Sante | Grand Total |
|---------|------|------------|-------------|
| FATOUA | 3 | 27 | 30 |
| KASUGHO | 7 | 23 | 30 |
| MBUHI | 11 | 19 | 30 |
| ALL | 21 | 69 | 90 |

### 7.8.4. Family Planning Benefits

General opinion amongst 71 of the 90 respondents was that there were significant benefits for women from family planning.

The main benefit considered (Table 6.07) was that women's health could be better maintained if they did not have so many children.

Table 6.07 What benefits from family planning

| Village | No perceived benefits | DM | Economic | Female Health |
|---------|-----------------------|-----|----------|---------------|
| FATOUA | 9 | 1 | 1 | 19 |
| KASUGHO | 6 | | 2 | 22 |
| MBUHI | 5 | | 1 | 24 |
| ALL | 20 | 1 | 4 | 65 |

Just over 20% of respondents did not consider that there were any real benefits from family planning.

### 7.8.5. HIV and STD

Households had some access to advice about HIV and other STD (Table 6.08). 80% of respondents said that they had received some information.

Table 6.08 Advice on HIV and STD

| Village | % with access to advice |
|---------|-------------------------|
| FATOUA | 76.67 |
| KASUGHO | 76.67 |
| MBUHI | 86.67 |
| ALL | 80.00 |

Once again the important role of the village health post/clinic is illustrated. From the results in table 6.09, 48 of 90 respondents indicated that the local clinic (post santé) was their primary source of advice on HIV and STD.

**Table 6.09 Main source of advice on HIV and STD**

| Village | 0 | CBCA | CBCE | ECOLE | EGLISE | Post Sante | RADIO | RCT | RGT | VOISIN |
|---|---|---|---|---|---|---|---|---|---|---|
| FATOUA | 7 | 3 | | | 3 | 16 | | | 1 | |
| KASUGHO | 7 | | | 1 | 2 | 15 | 3 | 1 | | 1 |
| MBUHI | 4 | 1 | 2 | | 4 | 17 | 1 | | 1 | |
| ALL | 18 | 4 | 2 | 1 | 9 | 48 | 4 | 1 | 2 | 1 |

## 8.0. Attitude towards RGT

Respondents were asked if they thought that the establishment of the RGT was a good idea. Overwhelmingly over 92% though it was broadly positive move (Table 7.01)

**Table 7.01 Attitudes to the establishment of RGT (% of households)**

| Village | 1 Broadly positive | 2 Broadly Negative | 3 No idea |
|---|---|---|---|
| FATOUA | 80.00 | 10.00 | 10.00 |
| KASUGHO | 96.67 | 3.33 | 0.00 |
| MBUHI | 100.00 | 0.00 | 0.00 |
| ALL | 92.22 | 4.44 | 3.33 |

When further asked to clarify if the establishment of the reserve and the associated development projects might impact on their lives 90% of respondents said that they expected a beneficial impact from the development projects (Table 7.02).

**Table 7.02 Attitude to impact from development projects on household life (% of households)**

| Village | Improve life | No impact | no idea |
|---|---|---|---|
| FATOUA | 76.67 | 10.00 | 13.33 |
| KASUGHO | 96.67 | 0.00 | 3.33 |
| MBUHI | 96.67 | 0.00 | 3.33 |
| ALL | 90.00 | 3.33 | 6.67 |

These results are a good indication that the establishment of the reserve and the associated development activities are at the least clearly linked in peoples minds, and that there are high expectations regarding the future benefits from the development projects that have been discussed with local communities. Whilst these results do not explicitly indicate how people view the forest and future benefits from improved management, it does not seem likely that local communities have not bough into the process of establishing the community reserve because they value the forest in terms of conservation and sustainable management benefits.

In order to more fully appreciate the links between forest conservation and perceived livelihoods benefits, more extensive participatory and qualitative assessments would need to be made to answer questions about what aspects of life have changed and in and what ways. What remains to be seen is if people really feel the same way once they are effectively restricted in their access of the forest reserve.

## 9.0. Radio Listening

The radio can obviously be an important medium by which to educate listeners about various development or conservation issues. Across all villages 30% of respondents said that they did not listen to the radio (Table 8.01), presumably because they had no access to one.

**Table 8.01 Households listening to the radio**

| Village | yes | no | % not listening |
|---------|-----|-----|-----------|
| FATOUA | 18 | 11 | 36.67 |
| KASUGHO | 25 | 5 | 16.67 |
| MBUHI | 19 | 11 | 36.67 |
| ALL | 62 | 27 | 30.00 |

Of those households who listened to the radio regularly, 45.56% reported hearing about health issues as a main topic of interest. (Table 8.02)

**Table 8.02 Radio topics of main interest (%of households)**

| Village | HEALTH | Agriculture | Market prices | Development | Environment | Conservation |
|---------|--------|-------------|---------------|-------------|-------------|--------------|
| | yes | yes | yes | yes | yes | yes |
| FATOUA | 46.67 | 6.67 | 0.00 | 23.33 | 3.33 | 6.67 |
| KASUGHO | 53.33 | 26.67 | 6.67 | 36.67 | 13.33 | 20.00 |
| MBUHI | 36.67 | 13.33 | 3.33 | 30.00 | 16.67 | 13.33 |
| ALL | 45.56 | 15.56 | 3.33 | 30.00 | 11.11 | 13.33 |

## 10.0. Household Incomes

Analysis of income data (Table 9.01) showed that the average annual income over all villages was just over $1737. Various income variables are shown in table 9.01. Reported values may seem high. At this point it should be refreshed in our minds the difference between absolute and adjusted measures of income and that income measures include the value of own produced goods consumed, not just sold in the market (See above, section 1.0). The proportion of the value reported that is manifest as actual cash that the household sees is actually very low (up to10% of the reported value in most cases).

## 10.1. Total Income and Forest Income

Over all communities the average annual household income was just under $1740 and the adjusted value just over $464. Average annual income from forest goods was about $584 with the adjusted figure at about $154. On average across all villages mean adjusted income from the forest as a proportion of mean adjusted total income was 33.4%, showing that the forest provides an important source of goods to maintain local household's livelihoods.

**Table 9.01 Mean absolute and adjusted household income by village and mean % forest income as a share of total income.**

| Village (n) | Mean Total Income ($US) | Mean Forest Income ($US) | Mean Adjusted Total Income ($US) | Mean Adjusted Forest Income ($US) | Mean Adjusted Income from Forest as a % of Mean Adjusted Total income |
|---|---|---|---|---|---|
| FATOUA | 1898.78 | 501.45 | 563.64 | 149.37 | 26.50 |
| MBUHI | 1463.51 | 594.74 | 386.46 | 159.53 | 41.30 |
| KASUGHO | 1850.05 | 657.49 | 441.92 | 155.97 | 35.30 |
| ALL | 1737.45 | 584.56 | 464.01 | 154.96 | 33.40 |

## 10.2. Wealth and forest income

Analysis of income differences between wealth groups was conducted on the basis of income quartiles. Data was ordered according to adjusted total income and split into 4 quartiles, 1 having the lowest income and 4 having the highest. Mean total incomes and forest incomes were compared by quartiles

(Table 9.02). Unsurprisingly all categories of income were seen to increase with increasing income quartile. Interestingly mean adjusted income from the forest as a proportion of mean adjusted total income was seen to decrease with income quartile and this was highly significant (Kruskal Wallace—X = 17.560 d.f. = 3, p<0.01).

**Table 9.02 Household mean incomes, absolute and adjusted by income quartile**

| Income Quartile | Mean Total Income ($US) | Mean Forest Income ($US) | Mean Adjusted Total Income ($US) | Mean Adjusted Forest Income ($US) | Mean Adjusted Income From Forest as % of mean adjusted total income |
|---|---|---|---|---|---|
| 1 Lowest 25% | 714.97 | 395.53 | 172.53 | 96.49 | 55.93 |
| 2 | 1249.34 | 512.75 | 304.97 | 130.27 | 42.72 |
| 3 | 1859.34 | 701.64 | 507.09 | 186.08 | 36.70 |
| 4 Highest 25% | 3305.41 | 741.76 | 927.26 | 212.67 | 22.94 |
| ALL | 1737.45 | 584.56 | 464.01 | 154.96 | 33.40 |

The data show a clear relationship between increasing wealth and forest income. A linear regression model also supports this conclusion ($R^2$= 0.154, t = 4.001, p<0.001), however the low $R^2$ value indicates a lot of scatter (high variance). Thus that as households become wealthier they will not necessarily reduce their use of forests. In this case increasing incomes reduces the proportion that forest income contributes to overall income.

## 10.3. Consumption and sale of forest goods

Interestingly the majority forest products were sold for home consumption (Table 9.03), with only 0.17 % on average across all villages being sold, although this figure is biased upwards by the result from Fatoua.

**Table 9.03 Value of forest goods sold and consumed within the home**

| Village (n) | Mean value of forest goods sold US$ p.a. | Mean value forest goods consumed US$ p.a. | Mean total income from the forest US$ p.a. | Value of goods sold as % of mean total income from the forest |
|---|---|---|---|---|
| FATOUA | 33.17 | 468.28 | 501.45 | 6.62 |
| MBUHI | 11.85 | 582.89 | 594.74 | 1.99 |
| KASUGHO | 3.27 | 654.22 | 657.49 | 0.50 |
| ALL | 16.10 | 568.46 | 584.56 | 0.17 |

The difference between villages in the value of goods consumed was found to be significantly different between villages (Kruskal-Wallace, $X^2$ = 11.265, d.f. = 2, p<0.01)

An analysis by income quartiles also showed that there was a significant difference between income quartiles in terms of the value of forest goods sold, but this was still a very low proportion (2.75%) of the total value of forest good harvested.

**Table 9.04 Value of forest goods sold and consumed within the home by income quartile**

| Income Quartile | Mean value of forest goods sold US$ p.a. | Mean value forest goods consumed US$ p.a. | Mean total income from the forest US$ p.a. | Value of goods sold as % of mean total income from the forest |
|---|---|---|---|---|
| 1 Lowest 25% | 2.40 | 393.12 | 395.53 | 0.61 |
| 2 | 14.45 | 498.30 | 512.75 | 2.81 |
| 3 | 4.11 | 697.53 | 701.64 | 0.59 |
| 4 Highest 25% | 46.40 | 695.36 | 741.76 | 6.26 |
| ALL | 16.10 | 568.46 | 584.56 | 2.75 |

Thus by all wealth groups forest goods are used predominantly for home consumption and subsistence than for generating a cash income. Notably the highest income group (group 4) sold more forest produce than other income groups, but this difference was not found to be significant from other income groups, but there is no distinct trend in proportionate terms between forest goods sold and wealth.

## 10.4. Sources of forest income

Table 9.05 sets out some analysis of the values of different forest product categories. Values for all recorded product categories were totaled over all the sample, the total annual value of all product categories from the entire sample was calculated as $52, 563 (fifty two thousand five hundred and sixty-three USD). Fuel wood has the highest annual value of all the categories followed by small wild animals and then plants. In terms of consumption the almost all fuel wood is consumed within the home with plants (food, medicine and construction) being the next highest category.

Table 9.05 Value of forest product categories

| | Fuel wood and charcoal | Timber | Plants | Small Wild Animals | Larger Wild Animals | Mining |
|---|---|---|---|---|---|---|
| Annual Forest Income ($) | 45901 | 1067 | 2724 | 2669 | 125 | 77 |
| Forest Income Consumed ($) | 203 | 439 | 247 | 579 | 96 | 75 |
| Forest Income Consumed as % of total Forest Income | 45698 | 628 | 2477 | 2090 | 29 | 2 |
| Product category as share of total annual forest income (%) | 87.33 | 2.03 | 5.18 | 5.08 | 0.24 | 0.14 |

Larger wild animals formed a very small part of the total recorded bush meat. By Large animals we refer to antelopes, pangolins, monkeys and other primates. No elephants were recorded as bush meat. Small wild animals were porcupines, Gambian rats (cane rats) and other smaller rodents. More qualitative data on why small animals are targeted more than large animals is needed. Usually large animals often represent a better return per unit effort of hunting. However once large animals drop below a certain density, or become locally extinct, it becomes preferable to switch to other animals (usually smaller) that give a better return for hunting effort. In addition this may be resolved using biological data on animal densities in the buffer zones compared with those in less well exploited forest areas.

Timber was also of importance in the home; a significant portion of harvested wood was also sold but from what was reported the majority of timber exploitation was smaller trees for poles rather than sawn timber.

Clearly the biggest concern form a conservation perspective is the harvesting of fuel wood from forests. It is unlikely that the level of harvesting is sustainable at present. It is habitat loss through the collection of woody biomass for fuel and construction alongside conversion of forest to agricultural land that pose the greatest threat to conserving other biodiversity.

## 11.0. Conclusions

The study was conducted in one of the poorest areas of eastern DRC. People here have few opportunities to improve their livelihoods, access to markets is very poor, there are negligible opportunities for salaried or seasonal employment; people are inextricably dependent on the land and forests to maintain a subsistence lifestyle. Over the past ten years there has been little intervention to invest in development activities and the few activities have been hampered by constant insecurity, through outright civil war or from insurgents. The sample size was small and from a non random selection of communities in the region, therefore the results cannot be broadly applied to the regional population as a whole. However they may be typical of other communities of a similar size and geographic location.

The communities surveyed were comprised of households who in global terms were poor or ultra poor; this has serious implications for conservation. Poor households are likely to have limited economic alternatives and are more dependent on the protected area for their subsistence, or as an income source where wealthier people may use them to exploit the protected areas. Other research of regional relevance (Plumptre et al 2004) has also demonstrated that it is difficult for poor households to access locally available channels to improve their livelihood, e.g. the local CBOs credit and savings groups, whose membership tends to be socially stratified according to wealth and education. The poor are, thus, logistically excluded since they can't afford the conditions of membership. Therefore development activities must be well targeted towards specific socio-economic strata.

In addition if groups of people, such as the poorest households in the community, are both excluded from development activities and effectively excluded from forest resources upon which they have traditionally relied, they will be hit doubly hard. This will obviously lead to higher levels of disenfranchisement and increasingly negative views towards conservation amongst that group.

Creative methods of integrating poor people into the CCC development activities must be addressed. Poor people do not have the capital on which to take credit to finance their development activities. Social lending on the basis of a homogeneous group taking out loans together and being responsible for member to repay their loans is one way of overcoming the capital risk. Revolving funds of animals amongst homogeneous socio-economic groups can also be an effective means of increasing livestock numbers.

Community conservation through development activities will not in themselves protect the forest. Regional experience (Plumptre et al 2004) has shown that ICDP initiatives must work hand in hand with law enforcement and protection to be effective in combating unsustainable or illegal use of protected areas. ICDP serve to provide substitute means of maintaining and improving livelihoods and mitigating the potential conflicts between protected areas and local communities.

Potential insecurity is also a key issue related to the types of initiatives that are promoted. Clearly development interventions must be robust enough to with stand periods of insecurity, and also to not draw too much attention as a target for theft and looting. Concentrating on community level initiatives will mean that no one individual will be seen as being particularly wealthy, but the community management approach is fraught with potential management problems. Alternatively other social infrastructure such as community water points (boreholes/protected springs) can also have a profound impact on community welfare and would be robust against insecurity as the infrastructure (concrete) would not be attractive to theft. At a household level, investing in low cost interventions such as fruit trees, small stock (rabbits and guinea pigs) that can contribute to household nutrition and welfare, as well as in improving on household sanitation (basic pit latrines). Such interventions would also be of little potential value to looters.

## 12.0. The usefulness of the JGI BS

The best usefulness of a baseline study resides in its capacity to prepare for an impact evaluation of a given project. It's obvious that this exercise may be helpful for target settings and can be instrumental in selecting and tailoring activities at the project level.

Beside, this study has its own strengths and limitations which are still common in such particular settings.

## 12.1. Limitations of the baseline Study

- The baseline study does not provide information relating to the feeling of the population. Its design is seemingly quantitatively-oriented, and does not leave any space to the expression of feelings of surveyed population. A mix approach could be more meaningful.

- This baseline study is mainly activity—oriented: it does not tackle in depth realities behind potential intervention sectors. Nothing is said about the existence of Health Zones around the buffer zone of the community—based conservation area of Tayna.

- The baseline seems to be focused on a set of potential activities pre-selected by the team that conducted the baseline study.

- The baseline study does not provide any clear idea as to the level of poverty or of wealth. It rather provides a few items as proxy of wealth possessed by villagers. The use of proxy is a weakness common to studies conducted in villages.

- No idea is given by the study as to the level of insecurity. It could have been better to monitor the level of insecurity as security has to be seen as constraint to subsequent development interventions but also as basic reason of underdevelopment. In the second case, the project could be critical as it could help in curving insecurity by providing jobs to idle youth seen as easy target of rebellion movement. Nevertheless, a project that could bear hopes of lots of populations could end up in disappointing large chunk of the population as financial means allocated to development projects are always limited. Heavy expectations of populations may also undermine the sustainability of project interventions.

- The baseline study excludes possibility of conducting the Recalled Controlled Trials as no baseline is conducted within control zones. Yet the study confines any potential impact evaluation to the recourse to quasi—experimental designs.

- The lack of reliable statistics did not allow the use of statistically significant sample. The bases of sampling are unknown, and render difficult the utilization of sampling techniques. Therefore, the conclusions of the study cannot be rigorously extendable to the whole region of implementation of the project.

## 12.2. Areas of interest for Project implementers in the same Region

This BS is undoubtedly a very first investment of researchers' efforts in understanding dynamics of survival in the remote areas of the eastern DRC during a very challenging period of insecurity. It gives insights not only as to the economic aspects featuring this people living in the buffer zones of the community reserves, but also helps to understand the psychology of these populations fighting between insecurity and dire poverty.

## 12.2.1. Aspects to Highlight from the Baseline Study

1). <u>Community and household demography</u>—With stability and better administrative organisation managing a growing community becomes a more feasible task. Clearly a growing community need is land on which settle and provide for its members, and this will be a major challenge. Whilst the population density is perhaps not as high as in neighbouring regions i.e. Rwanda, there is a need to start the process of agricultural intensification to substitute for extensive agricultural practices in time. The demographic make-up suggests a lack of male household members amongst the key productive age groups which may be a significant constraint in the short term to local development (i.e. the ability of households to adopt certain technologies due to household labour constraints). This must be investigated, and the potential impact on the adoption of new technologies assessed, in order for development activities to be successful.

2). *Education*—This is one of the key long term factors in driving social and economic development. Cleary there is access to primary and secondary school education, and since the development of the University at Kasugho, tertiary education will in time become more accessible to people. It would be worth pursuing environmental and conservation education and awareness activities in schools to complement local ICD initiatives. This could comprise a practical as well as a theoretical element i.e. children can be involved in tree planting or other small local environmental management schemes.

3). <u>Employment</u>—Most people are employed in subsistence agriculture as the principal means of making a living. As suggested earlier, focusing on intensification of agriculture is imperative. In addition to agriculture a focus on other income generating activities is important; especially where households may rely on forest products e.g. bush meat to provide a source of income.

4). <u>Assets</u>—The low level of ownership of either livestock or other physical assets are clear indictors of poverty. As the general level of economic development increases we should see a corresponding increase in livestock, standard of housing, number of bicycles and radios etc. Development activities could focus on the provision of assets that are a means of making a living i.e. bicycles, sewing machines, agricultural implements etc. or that can improve the standard of living fuel e.g. fuel efficient stoves

5). <u>Association Membership</u>—a low proportion of households are association members. It is not clear from this study how well the associations identified actually function. Associations provide an efficient means of communicating information or organising training and it is worth pursuing partnership and synergies with existing associations and helping them work where possible. Otherwise a well-developed group development strategy to promote working together as a platform for association development might also be investigated.

6). <u>Credit</u>—There is poor access to credit, on any terms, and certainly credit on the basis of social capital was non-existent. Enterprise development requires capital to drive it and access to capital is a major barrier in the development of local enterprise. Credit can be very useful in providing opportunities for people to transform their livelihoods, ensuring that credit does just that and not simply get people indebted is challenging. As with other development activities crediting needs to be developed to meet different needs and targeted at different socio-economic groups.

7). <u>Environmental Resource Use</u>—There is a heavy reliance on environmental resources to sustain livelihoods i.e. land for agriculture, trees for fuel wood and building materials. In the case of natural forest, apart from introducing technologies that reduce the quantities of fuel wood that are consumed, some assessment of the biological sustainability must be made to help develop and idea of what level of use might be sustainable or to explore product substitution i.e. develop woodlots, aquaculture etc.

8). <u>Sanitation and Health</u>—Whilst there is a network of local clinics, anecdotal evidence shows that they are under resourced and badly supplied. However they remain the main focus for the majority of households on all aspects of health, family planning etc. On project health initiatives, the clinics are obviously a well-established entry point to the communities to promote health initiatives.

Promotion of improved latrines and education about how to clean drinking water are clearly necessary. In addition providing improved sources of drinking water through protecting springs, or digging borehole wells as an alternative to collecting drinking water from streams and rivers could also have a profound impact on well-being.

9). <u>Conservation Attitudes</u>—Little is known about local attitudes towards conservation, whilst many households feel that the establishment of RGT is broadly positive, this may well be because of anticipated benefits from associated development activities rather than from any desire to conserve the forest for future generations. More detailed qualitative assessment of the community forest relationship and the impact of restricted access on livelihoods and changes in attitudes as result is needed.

10).<u>Radio Listening</u>—The radio can be an important tool in disseminating ideas about conservation and development issues to the broad community. This type of adult education is important to broaden people's innate scope of what they might be able to achieve. It is no substitute for leadership and promotion of activities on the ground. Use of the radio needs to be closely aligned to field activities, so that if an issue is discussed on the radio, then people must be able to easily see or access the product, service or development program being discussed in order to get them to adopt it.

Any Implementing Agency may find pertinent and useful the above information deriving from the JGI baseline study for carrying out further potential programming. Yet the bulk of the above topics have become cross-cutting, and may inform any programming in post conflict settings. Following projects can use efficiently information taken from this baseline study:

- *Agriculture*—improve output of key crops and develop farming methods and understand key land resource constraints

- *Livestock*—schemes to improve livestock ownership and management i.e. revolving funds

- *Forestry*—encourage tree planting for fuel wood

- *Market access*—improve availability of transport, group marketing etc.

- *Health*—improvements to sanitation, potable water, family planning methods

- *Alternative Technologies*—Innovative approaches for fuel efficient stoves, biogas, green or solar stoves, etc.

Conducting a baseline study becomes a critical activity for Implementing Agencies in post-conflict settings as such exercise can reveal itself rewarding at a two-fold levels. Upward for setting targets of starting projects, selecting activities, and estimating levels of budgets required for carrying out targeted activities and downward for paving the way for rigorous impact evaluations. In post-conflict settings, as in any other settings, ideal evaluation reports will never be produced by evaluators due to the uniqueness of the projects' implementation. However, the most pertinent evaluation reports in post-conflict reports will be the ones capable to provide useful insights as to the efficiency and the effectiveness of the projects. The efficiency analysis would enable to understand whether the level of funding was sufficient whereas the effectiveness would help to understand whether the projects were able to reach their objectives. Such information is paramount for both implementing agencies and donors especially during current economic downturn context. Also, due to the globalization process supported by communication means capable to drive as quickly as possible tax payers' opinion. The same reasoning can apply on beneficiaries.

It's, therefore, advisable to arrange some co-funded baseline studies in post-conflict settings. Such initiatives have the advantage of reducing the cost of the studies due economies of scale while ensuring high quality reports. However, co-funding baseline studies would impose a high level of coordination among Implementing Agencies from the planning phase until the issuance of the final report of the baseline studies. This is feasible in a context of economic down turn as far as all stakeholders keep themselves engaged in development activities by throwing on the table their financial contributions, development expectations and by bringing their own contacts within country's carefully pre-selected.

N.B.: As the outcome of interest of this project was to contribute to reduction of deforestation, the baseline study should also have tackled the deforestation aspect. In fact, during the baseline study the level of forest coverage around the Tayna reserve was 89, 696 kilometers (2005) and during the closing out of the project was 89, 556.84 (2010). This means a forest loss of 0.16 percent, which is still low. The evaluation would just establish that the CCC project contributed to keeping the forest loss to a very low level of 0.16 percent.

### 12.2.2. How integrated is the Program

There are hence two ways of contemplating projects implemented in post conflict settings. The first approach consists in finding out whether a project is integrated since the very outset of the design of the project whereas the second consists in double-checking whether the project is linked to other projects implemented in the same region in a bid to produce sustainable results. While the first approach should be oversight by the Ministry of planning, the second should be led by the implementing agency. The latter should be eager to know whether the outcomes generated by the project can be attributed solely to the activities set in place by the project managers or there are other development actors in the region. Such awareness is even advisable due to the fact that synergies can be required in order to streamline resources (human and financial resources) in certain activities. Overlapping should be avoided at all costs as the economic context does not allow any waste of resources. Host countries and the donor community should invest the best of their efforts to address in an emergent mood issues relating to overlapping and waste of resources due to lack of on-the-ground coordination of implementing agencies. The implementation of the Busan declaration should put a strong emphasize on addressing similar issues. I do believe that by doing so, some additional resources may be pulled out in order to help more alleviating poverty-related issues. Obviously, to get there supposes a lot of effort of coordination among donors.

Fig 1. Coordination line in a post-conflict country

Weak coordination                    Strong coordination

Following various factors may influence donor coordination in a country struggling to step from conflict situation:

- The level of post-conflict situation of the country

- The government's willingness to collaborate and coordinate donors' effort toward reconstruction and development

- The convergence of interests among donors evolving in the country

- The geostrategic importance of the host country's stability in its region

It's obvious that the development agenda will be unveiled once the donor community reaches the strong coordination stage. At this very stage implementing agencies will contribute to the government's efforts aiming at moving the country towards certainties of socio-economic development. It's, therefore, the interest of the host country to work hard on the donor coordination agenda. Such efforts may be rewarding in terms of enabling a sound environment for donors' work and the same time help the country paving the way of development propelled by inside effort. It's important that members of the government understand that donors can't, by the virtue of their undertakings, develop the country.

# Chapter V

# Making Sense of Baseline Study Data

Baseline data are required for both impact and performance evaluation. Evaluations give characteristics of programs/projects and help to provide responses as to why given results were recorded by the monitoring system. Evaluations answers to the questions are we on good track or are we making some difference or changing something with our programs? Both types of questions lead to performance evaluation or impact evaluation. Both questions are useful in clarifying the issue of continuing the project the way it was designed or continuing the project the way we've been doing. In a context of economic crisis, donors will be very interested to know whether programs are making difference in people's lives or not.

## 4.1. Evaluation Maths

Usually, the evaluation issue will be reduced to the following mathematic reasoning:

Suppose that JGI decided to set in place a livelihood project providing to people living in the buffer zone of the community-based conservation areas with a livestock care training component (followed with small grants). We can estimate that the education (and grants) effects at the Mbuhi village level through comparisons of the pre and post-intervention (five years later) levels of each dependent variable among individuals in the treatment and control village samples. Using standard notation so that subscript **i** refers to an individual, subscript **t** refers to the time, and subscript **m** refers to the mbuhi village, we can formalize mathematically the income generated through the training as follows:

(1)  $Yimt = \beta ot + \beta_1 D_{it} + \beta_2 I_i + \beta_3 J_j + \epsilon_{im} t$

Where Dit represents prior exposure to the training moment with "0" value for all respondents at time t=1 and for control village respondents at time t=2, and with "1" for individuals in treatment villages only at time t=2; Ii represents all individual-level characteristics that are unique to individual I and that are stable over time, and Jm represents all stable village-level characteristics that are unique to the Mbuhi village, the $\beta$ represents regression coefficients linking the independent variables to the outcomes variable y, and $\epsilon$ is an error term. The equation models the individual's score on income improvement (Y) at a given point in time as a function of an overall average score for all individuals at that time $\beta ot$ plus some effect $\beta_1$ from having been exposed to the training session, along with effects from stable factors unique to each individual—either observed factors such as age or education level, or unobserved factors such as "personality"—and stable factors (e.g. observed socio-economic level or unobserved level of "social capital") unique to the village. This equation can be expressed for each individual in the treatment and control villages at both points in time, and an expression for the difference or change in income generated can be obtained by subtracting the equation at time 1 (before the session) from the equation at time 2 (after the session). This results in the following basic equation for estimating the effect of the treatment at the village level:

(2) $\text{Yim1} = \beta_{o1} + \beta_1 D_{i1} + \beta_2 I_i + \beta_3 J_m + \text{\euro}_{im1}$

$\text{Yim2} = \beta_{o2} + \beta_1 D_{i2} + \beta_2 I_i + \beta_3 J_m + \text{\euro}_{im2}$

$\Delta\text{Yim2} = \Delta\beta_{o2} + \beta_1 \Delta D_i + \beta_2 \Delta I_i + \beta_3 \Delta J_i + \text{\euro}_{im}$

Which, since the individual and village level i and m terms are assumed to be stable, reduces to the following basic estimation equation for assessing the effects of the training session:

(3) $\Delta\text{Yim} = \Delta\beta_o + \beta_1 \Delta D_i + \Delta\text{\euro}_{im}$

Alternatively, since $\Delta Di$ equals 0 for all individuals in the control villages and 1 for all individuals in treatment villages, the equation can be expressed as modelling the "difference in the average difference' in the dependent variable for the treatment and control villages:

(4) $\Delta\text{Yim} = \Delta\beta_o + \beta_1 \text{TREATMENTi} + \Delta\text{\euro}_{im}$

Where $\Delta\beta_o$ then represents the average change over time in income Y for control villages, and $\beta_1$ represents any additional change in y for individuals in treatment villages. If the $\beta_1$ coefficient is statistically significant, this indicates that the change in income (dependent variable) in treatment villages is statistically different from the change in control villages.

Similar reasoning is used in performance evaluation especially for summative evaluations.

## 4.2. Challenges with Performance Evaluation

Departing from descriptive and formative questions, performance evaluations will be needed in a bid to say whether the project is on good track or whether the project achieved what achieved what it was intended to. In the latter case, the evaluation is a summative one, and appeals for baseline data. In a sense, performance evaluations comprehend some impact aspects.

In post-conflict settings, following challenges may stand on the ways of evaluators:

1. **Lack of baseline data**: the implementation area was not secure during the start phase of the project. Failure to implement the project in the current insecurity context could have resulted in a humanitarian crisis. Recall techniques may be later on helpful for further evaluations.

2. **Lack of consensus among stakeholders on initial activities**: most of time project to be implemented in post-conflict settings would require a number of stakeholders including the local government, the traditional chief, and another local development organization. This is a typical mix of stakeholders which usually helps to avert misunderstandings. Though this mix may prove efficient in starting the project implementation, it can also prove difficult to allow initial studies to take place. These may be seen as a waste of time and resources by some stakeholders. Sharing the same values could be helpful among stakeholders as many implementing agencies would chose to skip on the baseline study step. Unfortunately,

financial interests don't always coincide with impact and efficiency interests around projects/programs.

3. **More focus is put on financial resources allocation rather than on achieving results**: the implementing agency is part of a consortium which is accountable for the lump sum of money allocated for achieving certain results, no matter how the results are achieved. This problem occurs when decision makers do not have tight oversight on project being implemented far away with very little activities' monitoring. Decision makers who allocate the money for the project implementation just wait for reports that they may read or not.

4. **Local government involvement in the project implementation**: it usually happens that local African countries including the Government of the Democratic Republic of the Congo operate out of managing for results principles. The lack of accountability could be exacerbated when the local government involvement via a ministry or any other government entity provides greater financial powers to the governmental party. In such a context, performance evaluations won't need baseline studies as establishing realistic results for accountability will never be part of the game.

### 4.3. Tools for gauging Impact of Development Projects

Post-conflict related situations have different phases. When a country is on the verge of quitting the post-conflict situation and get bound to development phase, some strategic choices have to be operated. In a bid to make this momentum productive, a results-based management approach should be adopted across the government services and institutions. Hence, policy-making should be evidenced-based with monitoring and evaluation as its hallmark. In a context of economic (and financial crisis) this requirement becomes demanding for both the country benefiting from aid and from the donor's country. The latter is keen to know whether development intervention' approaches are proving successful, and the first for consolidating its long way of progress towards development. In this very context, "*policy makers and civil society are demanding results and accountability from public programs, impact evaluation can provide robust and credible evidence on performance and, crucially, on whether a particular program achieved its desired outcomes. At the global level, impact evaluations are also central to building knowledge about the effectiveness of development programs by illuminating what does and does not work to reduce poverty and improve welfare*".[17]

By the virtue of its nature, the Impact Evaluation is very demanding in terms of design and methodology, data collection methods, and data analysis tools. Baseline data should have been collected since the very outset of the project design phase. Two approaches have been conflicting regarding the baseline. Some would like to simply ignore the baseline aspect at the beginning and think about it when it comes to create an impact evaluation strategy (retrospective impact evaluation supporters) while others argue that baseline data should be envisaged and collected since the very outset of the project i.e. at the design phase of the project (prospective impact evaluation supporters). In my sense, only

---

[17]    Paul J. Gertler et al: "Impact Evaluation in Practice", the World Bank, 2011, p. 4.

prospective evaluations are able to provide strong and credible counterfactuals which are really needed when it comes to decision making in post conflict settings.

That said, following difficulties will complicate the prospective evaluation approach in post conflict settings:

1.  Mobility of project beneficiaries and potential spill over effects: post-conflict areas usually face volatile security situations. People may spend two peaceful weeks and face serious instability after the couple of weeks of stability and so forth. Therefore, zones originally chosen as treatment zones may be hosting at the end of day many people from control zones. This situation should be carefully assessed as the project is being implemented in order to establish how alarming it could be to the whole process. The mid-term review is always a good opportunity to review the reliability of data to be following on towards a final impact evaluation. Sound qualitative tools may be highly helpful at this stage.

2.  Possible "Hawthorne effect": the "Hawthorne effect" happens when targeted population behave differently being aware that they are observed. In situation of dire poverty, some people would think that behaving in a different way may convince project managers to keep its project along with its benefits to the community. In such situation, project managers should start the project managing these rumours since the very beginning of project activities and set in place a communication strategy that can favour transparency and truthfulness.

3. Change of some key stakeholders' approach: it can happen that during the implementation of a project, one stakeholder decides to change the implementation area of the project for political reasons. This happens quiet often in post-conflict settings since the government, as key stakeholders, has always its own political interest in project implementation. While an impact evaluation is scheduled to take place sometimes at the end of the project, any change in the treatment zones may affect the whole evaluation process. In order to counter this aspect, the evaluation leader should bear in mind this possibility while designing the evaluation plan. This could be assuring more statistical power to the sample or make sure that other areas could be used in lieu of the ones officially contemplated as part of the treatment/control groups.

4. Ethic issues and local population's misunderstanding: ethics issues are well known in evaluation communities. The golden principle is that evaluation should follow the normal activities' implementation not the reverse. Evaluators should be driven by the need to answer to policy-makers' questions rather than by their own taste of learning like in chemistry or physics. Otherwise, evaluation studies will be seeking for increasing knowledge rather than improving people's welfare. This could be missing the real reason of evaluation as a tool for improving project managements, education tools, or reshaping public policies.

# CONCLUSION

Gathering detailed household information is a challenging task especially when it comes to post-conflict settings. Biases are unavoidable from various sources: recall bias from people surveyed and living in very poor areas; errors and misunderstanding from enumerators who always don't live in the same areas, and can't be as faithful as possible to traduce on papers surveyed people's realities. Various authors made sound suggestions to counter these limitations such as Velded who suggests making several visits once a quarter to a panel of households to build an accurate picture of income and consumption patterns. Whilst repeated visits are technically desirable, panel data collection can also be prohibitively expensive and time consuming especially in areas where security is volatile. Evaluators will have to weigh in all these factors and be able to come up with data that can be used to inform evaluations (mid-term or final reviews).

This study walked the reader also through challenges and ways to overcome the use of baseline studies for conducting real life evaluation in post-conflict settings. Therefore, the paradox of post-conflict countries pumping lots of financial resources in economic and financial crisis context, and whose impacts are not established would be fixed. Donor countries are submitted to very stringent standards of accountable, which should be applied and imposed to implementing agencies and states benefiting from donor communities. One of these standards is to make sure that projects are meeting their objectives as stated in their monitoring and evaluation plans agreed with donors and leave some impact in areas of interventions. The merit of this book is to present to evaluators and implementing agencies real challenges but also real opportunities to technically conduct baseline studies for evaluations. Despite security and technical concerns, baseline studies are still feasible. No implementing agency should be exonerated from conducting baseline studies and evaluations. The most important is to state clearly its methodology of study, challenges and ways of overcoming these challenges.

# BIBLIOGRAPHY

## I. BOOKS AND ARTICLES

1. Collier Paul et Anke Hoeffler: *"Green and grievance in civil war"*, Oxford Economic Papers, 2004

2. Collier Paul: *"Risk and Investment in Africa"*, Mcmillan, 2000

3. Mankiw Gregory: *"Macroeconomics",* Worth Publishers, New York, 2007

4. Gertler Paul et al: *"Impact Evaluation in practice"*, World Bank, 2011.

5. Linda G. Morra and Ray C. Rist: **"The Road to Results: designing and conducting effective development evaluations"**; World Bank, 2009.

6. African Development Bank. ***Results-Based Country Strategy Paper*. Kinshasa: African Development Bank**, April 2010.

7. Demetriou, Spyros and Salamah Magnuson. **"Strengthening United States Foreign Policy in the DRC."**

8. European Union. ***The EU's Support to Security System Reform in the DRC: Perceptions from the Field in spring* 2010**. Kinshasa: May 2011.

9. Government of the Democratic Republic of Congo. *Country Plan*, May 2008.

10. Government of the Democratic Republic of Congo, Ministry of Planning. *Kinshasa Agenda memo)*. Kinshasa: June 2009.

11. Government of the Democratic Republic of Congo, Ministry of Planning. *"Les Groupes Thématiques en Bref."* Kinshasa: No. 0018, 2011.

12. Government of the Democratic Republic of Congo, Ministry of Planning. *Poverty Reduction Strategy Paper II.* Kinshasa: November 2011.

13. United Nations Development Program. *"Evaluation des Résultats des Activités de Développement du PNUD en RDC."* Kinshasa: November 2011.

14. World Bank. *DRC's Country Assistance Framework*. Washington, DC: World Bank, May 2008

## II. <u>REPORTS</u>

1. Nathan Associates: *"Patterns of Post Conflict Economic Recovery: May 2009"*, Report to USAID, http://www.countrycompass.com,

2. African Development Bank: *"Mid-term Review of the Results-based Country Strategy Paper"*, 2010

3. More Sylvie and Megan Price: *"The European Union Support to Security System Reform in DRC: perceptions from the field in spring 2010",* 2011.

4. Bush Glenn and Mumbere Olivier: *"Baseline Study Report of the CCC Project",* 2005.

5. *UNICEF-RDC: "Eliminer la pauvreté: Objectifs du Millénaire pour le Développement 2015"*; Rapport Pays 2010

6. Wiater John: Food for the Hungry, *"Final Evaluation Report of the Multi-Year Assistance Program 2008-2011",* December 2010